A CHARGE TO KEEP

40-Lesson Bible Study on Renouncing Sin & Embracing Holiness

A CHARGE TO KEEP

40-Lesson Bible Study on Renouncing Sin & Embracing Holiness

Marcus E. Turner

Zarephath Press

Copyright © 2024 by Marcus E. Turner

A Charge to Keep

40-Lesson Bible Study on Renouncing Sin & Embracing Holiness

Published by Zarephath Press (ISBN 978-0-9799414-2-9)

All rights reserved. Printed in the United States of America

Dedicated to the memory of my late father, Robert L. Turner,
my mother, Hazel L. Turner,
my wife, Lisa S. Turner,
my four children, Marcus, Gabrielle, Victoria, and Bethany,
and my church, Beulah Baptist Church

Table of Contents

A Charge to Keep	1
The Charge	3
Accomplishing the Charge	7

LESSONS

1 – REPENT	9
2 – BE DISCIPLED	13
3 – YIELD YOUR LIFE TO GOD	17
4 – LIVE A PURE LIFE	21
5 – BE OBEDIENT TO GOD	25
6 – FOCUS ON THE RIGHT THINGS	29
7 – WATCH FOR & RESIST THE DEVIL	33
8 – STAY THE COURSE	37
9 – CHOOSE WISELY	41
10 – DEPEND ON GOD	45
11 – HEED TO WHAT IS RIGHT	49
12 – AVOID LETTING PRAISE DISTRACT	53
13 – NEVER FORGET GOD	57
14 – BE IN CHRIST	61
15 – CIRCUMVENT SADNESS	65
16 – RESPOND APPROPRIATELY	69
17 – BE DETERMINED TO SUCCEED	73
18 – GIVE WHOLEHEARTEDLY	77
19 – WALK WORTHY OF YOUR CALLING	81
20 – WALK DIFFERENTLY	85

21 – FOLLOW THE WAY OF THE EAGLE	89
22 – OBEY THE TRUTH	93
23 – BE RECEPTIVE TO GUIDANCE	97
24 – DISREGARD THE OPINIONS OF OTHERS	101
25 – BE UNCOMPROMISING	105
26 – ADHERE TO THE GOLDEN RULE	109
27 – DESIRE GOD'S PRESENCE	113
28 – GET BACK TO THE BASICS	117
29 – PRAISE GOD	121
30 – REHEARSE GOD'S HOLINESS	125
31 – DEAL WITH SIN BIBLICALLY	129
32 – ADD THE RIGHT THINGS TO YOUR LIFE	133
33 – FIGHT THE GOOD FIGHT OF FAITH	137
34 – BEWARE OF MISPLACED JOY	141
35 – SEEK RESTORATION	145
36 – SPEAK UP BOLDLY	149
37 – DEVELOP A DEEP HATRED OF THE WORLD	153
38 – ADHERE TO THE DEMANDS OF MINISTRY	157
39 – RESIST DESPISING STRUGGLES	161
40 – STAND FIRM	165

Perfecting Holiness   169

A Charge to Keep

The phrase "a charge to keep" resonates deeply within the biblical context, reflecting a sense of responsibility and stewardship that is woven throughout the Scriptures. In the Holy Bible, this concept can be traced back to various passages that emphasize the importance of fulfilling one's duties, whether they pertain to God, family, or community. The phrase itself suggests a commitment to uphold certain values and to act in accordance with divine expectations.

In the context of the song titled "A Charge to Keep," the lyrics echo the biblical call to live a life of purpose and integrity. The song serves as a reminder that each individual has been entrusted with specific responsibilities that align with their faith. This idea is beautifully illustrated in the parable of the talents found in Matthew 25:14-30, where servants are given resources to manage on behalf of their master. The expectation is clear: they are to use what they have been given wisely and productively, reflecting the trust placed in them.

Moreover, the concept of a charge to keep can also be linked to the Great Commission in Matthew 28:19-20, where Jesus instructs His followers to go forth and make disciples of all nations. This directive emphasizes the importance of actively engaging in the world, sharing the message of hope and salvation, and nurturing the spiritual growth of others. It highlights that our charge is not merely a personal endeavor but a collective mission that requires dedication and action.

In addition, the biblical perspective on stewardship extends to caring for creation and serving others. Genesis 2:15 speaks of humanity's role in tending to the Garden of Eden, symbolizing our responsibility to care for the earth and its inhabitants. This stewardship is echoed in the song, which calls for a commitment to live out our faith through acts of service and love.

Ultimately, "a charge to keep" encapsulates the essence of living a life that honors God and fulfills our responsibilities to one another. It challenges us to reflect on how we can actively engage in our communities, uphold our values, and contribute positively to the world around us. It serves as a reminder that with every charge comes the opportunity to make a meaningful impact, guided by faith and purpose.

The Charge

Renouncing sin and embracing holiness stands as the foremost calling for believers, as emphasized throughout the Holy Bible. This profound transformation is not merely a suggestion but a divine mandate that shapes the very essence of a believer's life. The Scriptures consistently highlight the importance of turning away from sinful behaviors and attitudes, urging followers of Christ to pursue a life that reflects His righteousness.

In the New Testament, the Apostle Paul articulates this charge with clarity. In Romans 12:1-2, he implores believers to present their bodies as living sacrifices, holy and pleasing to God. This act of surrender signifies a deliberate choice to reject worldly influences and sinful desires. It is a call to renew the mind, allowing the truth of God's Word to transform thoughts and actions. By doing so, believers align themselves with God's will, which is inherently good, pleasing, and perfect.

Moreover, the concept of holiness is woven throughout the Old Testament as well. In Leviticus 20:26, God commands His people to be holy because He is holy. This call to holiness is not about adhering to a set of rules but about cultivating a relationship with God that leads to a life marked by purity and righteousness. It involves a conscious decision to turn away from sin, recognizing its destructive nature and the separation it creates between humanity and God.

Embracing holiness also means reflecting the character of Christ in everyday life. Believers are called to be the light of the world, showcasing love, grace, and truth in their interactions. This pursuit of holiness is not a solitary journey; it is supported by the community of faith, where encouragement and accountability foster spiritual growth.

The call to forsake sin and wholeheartedly embrace holiness is a profound charge, guiding one toward a more intimate relationship with God. It is a lifelong commitment that not only impacts the individual believer but also serves as a powerful testimony to the world of God's redeeming love and grace.

Renounce Sin

Renouncing sin is a fundamental concept in the Christian faith, deeply rooted in the teachings of the Holy Bible. It signifies a conscious decision to turn away from sinful behaviors and attitudes, reflecting a believer's commitment to living a life that honors God. This act of renunciation is not merely about avoiding wrongdoing; it embodies a transformative process that aligns one's life with the principles of faith.

The Bible emphasizes the importance of renouncing sin in various passages. For instance, in 1 John 1:9, it states that if we confess our sins, God is faithful and just to forgive us and cleanse us from all unrighteousness. This verse highlights the relationship between acknowledging sin and receiving God's grace. By renouncing sin, believers open themselves to the transformative power of forgiveness, which is central to the Christian experience.

Moreover, renouncing sin is closely tied to the concept of repentance. In Acts 3:19, believers are called to repent and turn to God so that their sins may be wiped out. This turning away from sin is not a one-time event but a continual process that reflects a believer's growth in faith. It signifies a desire to align one's life with God's will, fostering a deeper relationship with Him. The significance of renouncing sin also extends to the community of believers. In Galatians 6:1, Paul instructs the church to restore those caught in sin gently, emphasizing the importance of accountability and support within the faith community. By renouncing sin collectively, believers create an environment that encourages spiritual growth and mutual encouragement.

Furthermore, the act of renouncing sin serves as a witness to the world. In Matthew 5:16, Jesus encourages His followers to let their light shine before others, that they may see their good deeds and glorify the Father in heaven. When believers actively renounce sin, they demonstrate the transformative power of faith, showcasing the difference that a life committed to Christ can make.

Ultimately, turning away from sin is an essential part of the Christian faith, intricately linked to the believer's spiritual path. This commitment requires a conscious decision to reject wrongdoing, seek repentance, and cultivate a nurturing community. As believers engage in this journey, they undergo profound personal change and become living examples of God's grace at work in the world.

Embrace Holiness

The pursuit of holiness stands as a fundamental principle throughout the Holy Bible, reflecting the profound significance it holds for believers. The concept of holiness is woven throughout Scripture, emphasizing that it is not merely an abstract idea but a vital aspect of a believer's life. To embrace holiness means to align oneself with God's character, which is inherently pure and righteous.

In the Old Testament, God calls His people to be holy as He is holy (Leviticus 11:44). This call is not just for the sake of separation from sin but is rooted in the relationship between God and His people. Holiness signifies a commitment to live according to God's standards, which fosters a deeper connection with Him. It is an invitation to experience the fullness of life that comes from walking in His ways.

The New Testament further expands on this theme, particularly through the teachings of Jesus and the Apostles. In 1 Peter 1:15-16, believers are reminded to be holy in all their conduct, echoing the call from Leviticus. This call to holiness is not about legalism but about transformation. When believers embrace holiness, they allow the Holy Spirit to work within them, shaping their thoughts, actions, and desires to reflect Christ's character.

Holiness is also closely tied to the concept of love. Jesus summarized the law and the prophets with the command to love God and love others (Matthew 22:37-40). Embracing holiness enables believers to love authentically, as it cultivates a heart that seeks to honor God and serve others selflessly. This love is a natural outflow of a life committed to holiness, demonstrating that true holiness is not isolation but active engagement in the world around us.

Moreover, embracing holiness has a communal aspect. The Church, as the body of Christ, is called to reflect God's holiness collectively. In Ephesians 4:1-3, Paul urges believers to live in a manner worthy of their calling, emphasizing unity and peace. When individuals within the Church embrace holiness, they contribute to a community that exemplifies God's love and grace, drawing others to Him.

Viewing holiness through a biblical lens and embracing it is essential for believers.

In conclusion, renouncing sin and embracing holiness is the primary calling for believers. It is the ultimate "Charge to Keep."

Accomplishing the Charge

Accomplishing a charge involves successfully executing a task or mission that has been assigned, often carrying an inherent sense of urgency and responsibility. This concept can be applied across various contexts, from military operations to spiritual responsibilities, and it emphasizes the importance of taking decisive action.

To begin with, direct action is a fundamental aspect of accomplishing the charge. It requires individuals to actively engage with their tasks rather than waiting for circumstances to align in their favor. This proactive approach is crucial, as it transforms intentions into tangible results. Whether it's a project at work, a personal goal, or a community initiative, taking the initiative to move forward is essential. This means breaking down the task into manageable steps, setting clear objectives, and maintaining focus on the end goal.

Responsibility plays a significant role in this process. When one takes ownership of a task, it fosters a sense of accountability that drives them to see it through to completion. This ownership can manifest in various ways, such as prioritizing the task, allocating necessary resources, and rallying support from others if needed. Embracing responsibility not only enhances personal growth but also builds trust and reliability among peers and stakeholders.

In a military context, the term "charge" evokes images of swift and bold maneuvers. Accomplishing the charge in warfare means executing a well-planned offensive strategy to overcome enemy positions. This requires not only courage but also meticulous planning and coordination. Soldiers must be trained to respond quickly and effectively, adapting to the dynamic nature of battle. The successful execution of such a charge can turn the tide of conflict, showcasing the importance of teamwork, strategy, and decisive action.

This book aims to clarify the biblical principles essential for fulfilling your spiritual responsibilities as a believer. The forty lessons, presented in a random sequence, will equip, motivate, instruct, and prepare you for the challenge ahead. The urgency of this charge serves as a powerful motivator, encouraging you to take action and achieve meaningful results. Seize this moment to transform your spiritual journey.

In Order to Renounce Sin and Embrace Holiness

1

You Must...

"REPENT"

In Order to Renounce Sin and Embrace Holiness

You must... "Repent"

2 Corinthians 7:10

Repentance is a powerful journey that enables individuals to distance themselves from sin and adopt a life of righteousness. At its essence, repentance requires a genuine recognition of our missteps and a sincere wish to change (2 Cor. 7:10). This journey transcends mere feelings of guilt; it involves understanding the repercussions of our actions and making a deliberate choice to pursue a more virtuous path.

When we truly engage in repentance, we unlock the door to renewal. This act of turning away from wrongdoing is similar to shedding an old layer, paving the way for spiritual growth and a stronger alignment with our core values. Embracing repentance signifies our readiness to face our imperfections, a challenging yet vital endeavor for personal growth. It prompts us to evaluate our decisions and grasp the effects they have on ourselves and those around us.

Additionally, repentance nurtures a sense of responsibility. By acknowledging our errors, we accept accountability for our actions, a fundamental step toward a more virtuous existence. This sense of responsibility not only aids us in renouncing sinful habits but also fortifies our determination to strive for holiness. It ignites a desire to align our lives with elevated principles and to seek forgiveness from ourselves and those we may have harmed.

As we embark on this life-changing path, we begin to develop virtues such as compassion, humility, and love. These traits are vital for a righteous life, steering us toward decisions that embody our commitment to goodness.

Ultimately, repentance is more than just a rejection of sin; it is an invitation to lead a life rich with purpose, integrity, and spiritual satisfaction. By embracing this transformative journey, we have the power to reshape our own lives and inspire others to embark on a similar path.

In Order to Renounce Sin and Embrace Holiness
you must... "Repent"

Here's an example...

A biblical character who demonstrates genuine and profound repentance is the prodigal son from Jesus' parable in Luke 15:11-32. The prodigal son, a young man, demands his inheritance and leaves his father's house to live a life of reckless indulgence. Eventually, he squanders all his wealth and finds himself in poverty, feeding pigs and yearning for the food they eat. In this moment of desperation, he realizes his sin and recognizes his unworthiness to be called a son, deciding to return to his father and seek forgiveness.

The prodigal son's repentance is a model of true humility and remorse. He acknowledges his wrongdoing, saying, "Father, I have sinned against heaven and against you. I am no longer worthy to be called your son" (Luke 15:18-19). His repentance is not just about regret over his circumstances but a heartfelt recognition of his offense against God and his father.

Upon returning, the father receives him with open arms, symbolizing God's boundless grace and forgiveness. This story exemplifies perfect repentance—turning from sin, acknowledging fault, and humbling oneself before God with a contrite heart. It highlights the transformative power of repentance and God's readiness to forgive.

Here's some practical steps...

- Understand the concept of repentance as a change of heart and mind.
- Acknowledge your sins and take responsibility for your actions.
- Confess your sins to God sincerely and openly.
- Seek forgiveness through prayer, asking God to cleanse you.
- Turn away from sinful behaviors and make a commitment to change.
- Study Scripture to understand God's will for your life.
- Cultivate a relationship with God through regular prayer and worship.
- Surround yourself with a supportive community of believers.
- Reflect on the consequences and repercussions of sin.
- Embrace the grace and mercy offered through Jesus Christ.

Journal Your Thoughts

In Order to Renounce Sin and Embrace Holiness

2

You Must...

"BE DISCIPLED"

In Order to Renounce Sin and Embrace Holiness

you must... "Be Discipled"
Matthew 28:19-20

Discipleship is a powerful journey that plays a crucial role in turning away from sin and embracing a life of holiness. When individuals commit to being discipled, they step into a nurturing environment designed for spiritual growth and learning. This journey often includes mentorship, accountability, and the sharing of personal experiences, all of which are essential for deepening one's faith.

One of the most significant advantages of discipleship is the chance to delve deeper into Scripture. As disciples come together to study the Bible, they uncover profound truths that illuminate their lives and help them understand the essence of sin. This understanding empowers them to identify sinful behaviors and motivates them to pursue transformation. The more they engage with God's Word, the clearer their path to holiness becomes.

Furthermore, discipleship cultivates a strong sense of community. Being part of a group of believers who are also dedicated to living righteously creates an encouraging and supportive atmosphere. This sense of belonging alleviates feelings of isolation that often accompany struggles with sin. By sharing their challenges and triumphs, individuals inspire one another to actively seek righteousness. Accountability partners play a vital role in this process, helping each other stay focused and resist temptation.

Additionally, discipleship emphasizes the practical application of faith. Through engaging discussions and activities, individuals learn how to integrate biblical principles into their everyday lives. This hands-on approach equips them with the necessary tools to make choices that reflect their commitment to holiness. As they practice these principles, they cultivate new habits that replace old, sinful patterns.

Ultimately, being discipled is an essential part of the journey toward holiness. It offers the knowledge, community, and practical support needed to turn away from sin and develop a life that mirrors God's character. Embracing this transformative process can lead to significant spiritual growth and renewal, fulfilling the call to make disciples of all nations as instructed in Matthew 28:19-20.

In Order to Renounce Sin and Embrace Holiness
you must... "Be Discipled"

Here's an example...

One prominent biblical character who was discipled is Timothy, a young leader in the early church. He was mentored and instructed by the Apostle Paul, who took him under his wing and helped shape him into a faithful servant of Christ. In 2 Timothy 1:5, Paul reminds Timothy of the faith that first lived in his grandmother Lois and his mother Eunice, showing the influence of a godly family. However, it was Paul's intentional discipling that equipped Timothy for ministry.

Paul not only taught Timothy the gospel but also modeled a life of perseverance, devotion, and spiritual discipline. In 1 Timothy 4:12, Paul encourages Timothy to set an example for others despite his youth, saying, "Don't let anyone look down on you because you are young, but set an example for the believers in speech, in conduct, in love, in faith and in purity." Paul invested time in Timothy, sending him to various churches to lead and guide believers, as seen in Philippians 2:22, where Paul calls Timothy "a son with the father."

Timothy's life illustrates the importance of spiritual mentorship. Through Paul's discipling, Timothy grew in faith and leadership, demonstrating how intentional discipleship can transform and equip believers for effective ministry.

Here's some practical steps...

- Explore the concept of discipleship as presented in the Holy Bible.
- Understand the importance of following Jesus' teachings and example.
- Engage in regular prayer and seek guidance from the Holy Spirit.
- Study Scripture diligently to deepen your understanding of God's Word.
- Participate in a community of believers for support and accountability.
- Embrace humility and a willingness to learn from others.
- Apply biblical principles in daily life to reflect Christ's character.
- Share your faith and experiences with others to encourage growth.
- Seek mentorship from mature Christians for personal development.
- Commit to lifelong learning and spiritual growth through discipleship.

Journal Your Thoughts

In Order to Renounce Sin and Embrace Holiness

3

You Must...

"YIELD YOUR LIFE TO GOD"

In Order to Renounce Sin and Embrace Holiness

you must… "Yield Your Life to God"

Romans 6:11-13

Embracing a life dedicated to God is an empowering expedition that can significantly alter your connection with sin and righteousness. By relinquishing your personal ambitions and desires for a greater purpose, you invite divine wisdom and strength into your life. This act of surrender is not just a singular choice; it represents an ongoing dedication to harmonizing your life with God's values and teachings. The primary teaching of Romans 6:11-13 emphasizes the importance of considering oneself dead to sin and alive to God, urging believers to offer their bodies as instruments of righteousness rather than yielding to sinful desires.

As you cultivate a deeper relationship with God through prayer, Scripture, and community, you begin to see the world through a different lens. The more you immerse yourself in His presence, the more you become aware of the areas in your life that need change. This awareness is the first step toward renouncing sin. You start to recognize the destructive patterns and habits that keep you from experiencing true joy and fulfillment. With God's help, you can confront these issues head-on, finding the courage to let go of what no longer serves you.

Embracing holiness becomes a natural outcome of this surrender. As you yield to God, you invite His spirit to work within you, transforming your heart and mind. Holiness is not about perfection; it's about striving to reflect God's love and grace in your daily life. You begin to develop a desire for righteousness, seeking to live in a way that honors God and uplifts those around you.

On this journey, you will face obstacles and difficulties, but surrendering to God grants you the strength to rise above them. With every step you take, your relationship with Him strengthens, and your dedication to turning away from sin intensifies. In the end, giving your life to God becomes a transformative force for embracing holiness, resulting in a life rich with purpose, tranquility, and deep-seated joy.

In Order to Renounce Sin and Embrace Holiness
you must... "Yield Your Life to God"

Here's an example...

A powerful example of a biblical character who yielded their life to God is the prophet Isaiah. In Isaiah 6, the prophet has a profound encounter with God that marks the turning point of his life and ministry. In this vision, Isaiah sees the Lord seated on His throne, surrounded by seraphim, and hears the heavenly declaration, "Holy, holy, holy is the Lord Almighty; the whole earth is full of his glory" (Isaiah 6:3). In response to this divine revelation, Isaiah is overwhelmed by his own sinfulness, exclaiming, "Woe to me! I am ruined! For I am a man of unclean lips, and I live among a people of unclean lips" (Isaiah 6:5).

However, God purifies Isaiah by sending a seraph to touch his lips with a burning coal, declaring that his guilt is taken away. It is at this moment that God asks, "Whom shall I send? And who will go for us?" Isaiah responds with complete surrender, saying, "Here am I. Send me!" (Isaiah 6:8).

Isaiah's willingness to yield his life to God's calling, despite the challenges of the prophetic mission ahead, exemplifies a heart wholly dedicated to God's purposes. His life became a testament of faithful obedience, offering his voice and life in service to God's will, no matter the cost.

Here's some practical steps...

- Understand the concept of surrendering to God as outlined in Scripture.
- Study relevant Bible verses that emphasize yielding one's life to God.
- Pray for guidance and a willing heart to submit to God's will.
- Reflect on personal desires and how they align with God's purpose.
- Seek to develop a relationship with God through regular prayer and worship.
- Acknowledge the importance of faith in trusting God's plan for your life.
- Commit to following biblical teachings and living according to the Bible.
- Engage in fellowship with other believers for support and encouragement.
- Practice humility and recognize the need for God's grace in your life.
- Continuously evaluate and adjust your life choices to align with God.

Journal Your Thoughts

IN ORDER TO RENOUNCE SIN AND EMBRACE HOLINESS

4

You Must...

"LIVE A PURE LIFE"

IN ORDER TO RENOUNCE SIN AND EMBRACE HOLINESS
YOU MUST... "LIVE A PURE LIFE"
Psalm 119:9-16

Living a pure life is a journey of profound change that can significantly aid in renouncing sin and embracing holiness. The passage from Psalm 119:9-16 emphasizes the importance of adhering to God's Word and commandments as a means to maintain purity and find joy in His teachings. When we commit to purity, we create a foundation for spiritual growth and moral clarity. This commitment involves not just abstaining from harmful behaviors but also cultivating positive habits that align with our values and beliefs.

A pure life encourages mindfulness in our thoughts, actions, and interactions with others. By focusing on what is virtuous and good, we begin to distance ourselves from temptations that lead to sin. This shift in focus allows us to recognize the beauty in living righteously, fostering a deeper connection with our spiritual selves. As we engage in practices such as prayer, meditation, and acts of kindness, we reinforce our commitment to holiness and develop a greater sense of purpose.

Moreover, living a pure life often involves surrounding ourselves with like-minded individuals who support our journey. This community can provide encouragement and accountability, making it easier to resist negative influences. When we share our experiences and struggles with others who are also striving for purity, we create a powerful network of support that strengthens our resolve.

Additionally, embracing purity can lead to a profound sense of peace and fulfillment. As we let go of sinful habits and embrace a life of integrity, we experience a lighter spirit and a clearer conscience. This inner peace is a reflection of our alignment with higher values and a deeper understanding of our purpose in life.

In conclusion, living a pure life is not merely about avoiding sin; it is about actively choosing to embrace holiness. By fostering positive habits, surrounding ourselves with supportive communities, and seeking inner peace, we can transform our lives and draw closer to a state of spiritual fulfillment.

IN ORDER TO RENOUNCE SIN AND EMBRACE HOLINESS
YOU MUST... "LIVE A PURE LIFE"

Here's an example...

One biblical character who exemplified purity of life is Joseph, the son of Jacob and Rachel, whose story is told in the Book of Genesis. Joseph's purity is particularly evident in his moral integrity, even in the face of intense trials. As a young man, Joseph was sold into slavery by his jealous brothers and taken to Egypt. There, he worked in the house of Potiphar, an Egyptian officer. Potiphar's wife attempted to seduce Joseph, but he refused, saying, "How then could I do such a wicked thing and sin against God?" (Genesis 39:9). His commitment to purity and righteousness led him to resist temptation, despite the personal cost, as he was falsely accused and imprisoned for his refusal.

Joseph's purity is not limited to his sexual integrity; it extends to his overall character. Even in prison, he maintained a spirit of honesty, humility, and faithfulness to God. Ultimately, Joseph's purity and steadfast trust in God's plan led to his rise to a position of great authority in Egypt, where he was able to save his family and many others during a time of famine.

Joseph's life serves as a powerful example of maintaining purity, righteousness, and faithfulness, even in the most challenging circumstances.

Here's some practical steps...

- Understand the importance of purity as outlined in Scripture.
- Study biblical passages that emphasize moral integrity and righteousness.
- Practice self-control and discipline in thoughts and actions.
- Surround yourself with positive influences and supportive community.
- Engage in regular prayer and meditation on God's Word.
- Avoid situations and media that promote impurity or temptation.
- Seek forgiveness and repentance when falling short of purity.
- Cultivate a heart of gratitude and humility before God.
- Serve others and focus on acts of kindness and love.
- Trust in God's strength to help maintain a pure lifestyle.

Journal Your Thoughts

IN ORDER TO RENOUNCE SIN AND EMBRACE HOLINESS

5

You Must...

"BE OBEDIENT TO GOD"

In Order to Renounce Sin and Embrace Holiness

you must... "Be Obedient to God"
1 Peter 1:14

Obedience to God, as highlighted in 1 Peter 1:14, acts as a strong driving force for renouncing sin and embracing a life of holiness. When we commit ourselves to following God's commands, we align our hearts and minds with His divine will, creating a foundation for spiritual growth and transformation. This alignment is crucial because it shifts our focus from worldly desires to a higher purpose, allowing us to see sin for what it truly is—a barrier to our relationship with God.

Being obedient means actively choosing to live according to God's principles, which often requires us to make difficult decisions. It involves a conscious effort to turn away from behaviors and thoughts that do not reflect His character. This process of renunciation is not merely about avoiding sin; it's about cultivating a deep-seated desire for holiness. As we immerse ourselves in God's Word and seek His guidance through prayer, we begin to understand the beauty of a life lived in accordance with His will.

Additionally, obedience cultivates a feeling of responsibility. When we recognize that our actions have spiritual implications, we become more mindful of our choices. This awareness empowers us to resist temptations that lead us astray. The more we practice obedience, the more we develop a distaste for sin, which can often seem appealing in the moment but ultimately leads to emptiness and regret.

Embracing holiness is a journey that requires perseverance and commitment. It's about allowing God to transform us from the inside out. As we grow in our relationship with Him, we find that our desires begin to change. We start to crave righteousness and seek to reflect God's love and grace in our interactions with others.

In essence, obedience to God is not just a duty; it is a pathway to true freedom. By renouncing sin and embracing holiness, we step into the abundant life that God has designed for us, filled with purpose, joy, and peace.

In Order to Renounce Sin and Embrace Holiness
you must... "Be Obedient to God"

Here's an example...

A striking example of obedience to God is found in the life of Abraham, particularly in his willingness to obey God's command to sacrifice his son, Isaac. In Genesis 22, God tests Abraham's faith by asking him to offer his beloved son as a burnt offering. Despite the immense emotional and spiritual difficulty, Abraham obeys without hesitation. Early the next morning, he sets out with Isaac to the mountain God had designated, fully intending to follow through with the command.

When Isaac questions why they are preparing the altar without a lamb for the sacrifice, Abraham responds, "God himself will provide the lamb for the burnt offering, my son" (Genesis 22:8). This statement reflects his trust in God's provision and his unwavering obedience. As Abraham is about to sacrifice Isaac, God intervenes, stopping him and providing a ram as a substitute.

Abraham's obedience in this moment exemplifies profound faith and trust in God's will, even when the command seemed incomprehensible. God rewards Abraham's obedience by reaffirming His covenant, promising that Abraham's descendants will become a great nation (Genesis 22:16-18). Abraham's life is a model of obedience, illustrating that true faith involves surrendering one's will to God, trusting His plan, and acting in obedience even in difficult circumstances.

Here's some practical steps...

- Understand the importance of obedience as a fundamental aspect of faith.
- Study biblical passages that emphasize obedience.
- Recognize that obedience involves both godly actions and attitudes.
- Pray for guidance and strength to follow God's commandments faithfully.
- Reflect on the teachings of Jesus as a model for living in obedience to God.
- Engage in regular Bible study to deepen understanding of God's expectations.
- Surround yourself with other Christians to gain encouragement and support.
- Acknowledge the role of the Holy Spirit in empowering you to obey God.
- Practice humility and repentance when falling short of God's standards.
- Commit to a lifestyle of obedience as a demonstration of devotion to God.

Journal Your Thoughts

In Order to Renounce Sin and Embrace Holiness

6

You Must...

"FOCUS ON THE RIGHT THINGS"

In Order to Renounce Sin and Embrace Holiness

you must... "Focus on the Right Things"
1 Peter 1:13

Focusing on the right priorities is essential for anyone seeking to renounce sin and embrace a life of holiness. When we direct our attention toward positive, uplifting pursuits, we create an environment that fosters spiritual growth and moral integrity, as highlighted in 1 Peter 1:13. By concentrating on what truly matters—such as love, compassion, and service to others—we naturally distance ourselves from temptations that lead to sin.

To begin with, setting our sights on virtuous goals helps us cultivate a mindset that values righteousness over wrongdoing. When we engage in activities that promote kindness and understanding, we reinforce our commitment to living a holy life. This shift in focus not only strengthens our resolve but also enhances our ability to resist negative influences. Surrounding ourselves with like-minded individuals who share our aspirations can further bolster our determination to pursue holiness.

Moreover, dedicating time to spiritual practices such as prayer, meditation, and studying Scriptures can deepen our connection to the Lord. These practices serve as reminders of our higher purpose and the values we strive to embody. By immersing ourselves in spiritual nourishment, we equip ourselves with the tools necessary to combat the allure of sin. The more we invest in our spiritual well-being, the more resilient we become against the distractions that threaten to derail our journey.

Additionally, focusing on gratitude and appreciation for the blessings in our lives can transform our perspective. When we acknowledge the goodness around us, we cultivate a sense of contentment that diminishes the desire for sinful indulgences. This shift in mindset allows us to find joy in living a life aligned with our values, rather than seeking fleeting pleasures that ultimately lead to regret.

In conclusion, by prioritizing the right things—such as love, spiritual growth, and gratitude—we empower ourselves to renounce sin and embrace a life of holiness. This intentional focus not only enriches our own lives but also positively impacts those around us, creating a ripple effect of goodness in the world.

IN ORDER TO RENOUNCE SIN AND EMBRACE HOLINESS
YOU MUST... "FOCUS ON THE RIGHT THINGS"

Here's an example...

A biblical character who exemplified focusing on the right things is the Apostle Paul. Throughout his ministry, Paul consistently kept his eyes fixed on the mission of spreading the gospel, regardless of the challenges and hardships he faced. In Philippians 3:13-14, Paul writes, "Brothers and sisters, I do not consider myself yet to have taken hold of it. But one thing I do: Forgetting what is behind and straining toward what is ahead, I press on toward the goal to win the prize for which God has called me heavenward in Christ Jesus."

Paul's focus was never on personal success, wealth, or comfort, but on the advancement of God's kingdom. He endured persecution, imprisonment, shipwrecks, and countless other trials, yet he remained undistracted from his mission. Even when others sought to discredit him or lead believers astray, Paul focused on teaching truth and encouraging the churches he planted to remain faithful to the gospel.

Paul emphasized the importance of focusing on eternal things over earthly matters, urging believers to set their minds on Christ. Paul's life is a model of prioritizing God's calling above all else, demon-strating that a Christ-centered focus brings lasting purpose and joy, regardless of life's difficulties.

Here's some practical steps...

- Understand the importance of prioritizing spiritual growth.
- Read and meditate on Scripture regularly.
- Pray for guidance and wisdom in daily decisions.
- Surround yourself with positive influences and community.
- Identify distractions that lead you away from faith.
- Practice gratitude to shift focus to blessings.
- Serve others to cultivate a Christ-like attitude.
- Reflect on Jesus' teachings and apply them to life.
- Set specific goals that align with biblical values.
- Trust in God's plan and seek His will in all things.

Journal Your Thoughts

In Order to Renounce Sin and Embrace Holiness

7

You Must...

"WATCH FOR & RESIST THE DEVIL"

In Order to Renounce Sin and Embrace Holiness

you must... "Watch For & Resist the Devil"

1 Peter 5:8-9

According to 1 Peter 5:8-9, resisting the devil and being vigilant against his temptations is crucial for anyone seeking to renounce sin and embrace a life of holiness. The first step in this journey is awareness. By recognizing the subtle ways in which the devil can influence thoughts and actions, individuals can better prepare themselves to resist these negative impulses. This vigilance allows one to identify moments of temptation before they escalate into sinful behavior.

When you actively watch for the devil's schemes, you cultivate a mindset that prioritizes spiritual growth. This proactive approach encourages you to fill your mind with positive, holy thoughts and to engage in practices that strengthen your faith. Prayer, meditation, and studying Scripture are powerful tools that not only fortify your spirit but also create a barrier against the devil's attempts to lead you astray. By immersing yourself in these practices, you develop a deeper relationship with the Lord, which in turn empowers you to reject sin.

Resisting the devil also demands a dedication to being accountable. Surrounding yourself with a supportive community of like-minded individuals can provide encouragement and strength. When you share your struggles and victories with others, you create an environment where holiness is celebrated, and sin is confronted. This communal aspect of faith reinforces your resolve to live a life aligned with your spiritual values.

Ultimately, the act of resisting the devil is not just about avoiding sin; it is about actively choosing holiness. Each time you successfully resist temptation, you strengthen your character and deepen your commitment to a righteous path. This continuous struggle against evil is a transformative journey that deepens your faith and enriches your spiritual life. By embracing this path, you will not only turn away from sin but also encourage others to seek holiness with you.

In Order to Renounce Sin and Embrace Holiness
you must... "Watch For & Resist the Devil"

Here's an example...

A compelling example of a biblical character who resisted the devil is Jesus Christ, particularly during His temptation in the wilderness. In Matthew 4:1-11, after Jesus was baptized, He was led by the Holy Spirit into the desert to be tempted by the devil. Over the course of forty days and nights, Jesus fasted and was physically weak, yet He remained spiritually strong. The devil approached Him with three temptations, each aimed at exploiting His human weaknesses.

The first temptation was for Jesus to turn stones into bread, to satisfy His hunger. Jesus resisted, quoting Scripture: "Man shall not live on bread alone, but on every word that comes from the mouth of God" (Matthew 4:4). The second temptation was for Jesus to throw Himself down from the pinnacle of the temple, testing God's protection. Jesus responded, "Do not put the Lord your God to the test" (Matthew 4:7). The third temptation offered Jesus all the kingdoms of the world in exchange for worship. Jesus rejected this with the command, "Worship the Lord your God, and serve him only" (Matthew 4:10).

Through each temptation, Jesus relied on Scripture and His obedience to God, resisting the devil's schemes. His victory over temptation serves as a model for believers, demonstrating the power of God's Word and steadfast faith in resisting evil.

Here's some practical steps...

- Understand the importance of spiritual armor as described in Eph. 6:10-18.
- Recognize that resisting the devil requires prayer and reliance on God.
- Study Scripture to know God's truth and counter the lies of the enemy.
- Practice humility, by submitting to God before resisting the devil (Jms. 4:7).
- Stay vigilant and aware of the devil's schemes, as mentioned in 1 Peter 5:8.
- Engage in regular worship and fellowship to strengthen your faith.
- Use the name of Jesus as a powerful tool against spiritual attacks.
- Focus on the promises of God to build confidence in His protection.
- Avoid temptation by fleeing from situations that may lead to sin.
- Maintain a lifestyle of repentance and seek forgiveness daily.

Journal Your Thoughts

In Order to Renounce Sin and Embrace Holiness

8

You Must...

"STAY THE COURSE"

In Order to Renounce Sin and Embrace Holiness

you must... "Stay the Course"

Psalm 119:1-8

Maintaining your spiritual path is crucial for turning away from sin and embracing a life of holiness. This journey demands dedication, resilience, and a profound understanding of your core values and beliefs. When you commit to staying true to your faith, you establish a solid foundation that empowers you to resist the temptations and distractions that can lead you astray.

Engaging regularly in practices like prayer, meditation, and the study of Scriptures deepens your connection with the Lord. This relationship not only fortifies your determination but also equips you with the wisdom and insight necessary to face life's obstacles. As you delve into these spiritual practices, you start to see sin for what it truly is—a temporary distraction that ultimately results in emptiness.

Additionally, remaining steadfast in your journey cultivates a sense of accountability. Being part of a supportive community of individuals who share your values encourages you to maintain your commitment to holiness. By discussing your challenges and triumphs with others, you create a nurturing environment that fosters collective growth, reinforcing your resolve to lead a life that aligns with your principles.

As you continue on this path, you will discover that renouncing sin becomes increasingly instinctive. The more you concentrate on embodying holiness, the less attractive sinful actions appear. This transformation may be gradual, but it is deeply impactful, as you begin to experience the joy and fulfillment that arise from living a life of integrity and purpose.

Ultimately, staying the course involves making a deliberate choice each day to prioritize your spiritual development. It's a pledge to consistently seek out what is good, true, and beautiful, allowing you to embrace a life that mirrors your highest aspirations. In doing so, you not only turn away from sin but also motivate others to embark on their own journeys toward holiness, echoing the sentiments of Psalm 119:1-8, which celebrates the blessings of walking in the ways of the Lord.

In Order to Renounce Sin and Embrace Holiness
you must... "Stay the Course"

Here's an example...

A powerful example of a biblical character who stayed the course is the prophet Daniel. Despite facing immense challenges, Daniel remained steadfast in his faith, consistently honoring God even when surrounded by foreign cultures, threats, and temptations. Taken captive by the Babylonians as a young man, Daniel could have compromised his beliefs to assimilate into the culture, but instead, he chose to remain faithful to God's commands. In Daniel 1:8, it says, "But Daniel resolved not to defile himself with the royal food and wine..." His commitment to purity and obedience set the tone for his entire life.

Daniel's perseverance is also evident in his unwavering devotion to prayer. In Daniel 6, when a decree was issued forbidding prayer to anyone except King Darius, Daniel continued to pray three times a day as he always had. Even when faced with the threat of the lion's den, Daniel refused to abandon his practice of seeking God's presence. God delivered him from the lions, demonstrating that faithfulness to God leads to His protection and favor.

Through decades of service in Babylon, Daniel remained committed to God's purposes, interpreting dreams, offering wisdom, and serving multiple kings. His life is a powerful testimony to staying the course in faith, regardless of trials or opposition.

Here's some practical steps...

- Understand the importance of faith in staying the course.
- Regularly read and meditate on Scripture for guidance.
- Pray consistently for strength and direction.
- Seek fellowship with other believers for support and encouragement.
- Embrace God's promises as motivation to persevere.
- Reflect on biblical examples of endurance and faithfulness.
- Practice obedience to God's commandments in daily life.
- Trust in God's timing and plan, even during challenges.
- Maintain a heart of gratitude to foster resilience.
- Share your journey and struggles with others to build accountability.

Journal Your Thoughts

In Order to Renounce Sin and Embrace Holiness

9

You Must...

"CHOOSE WISELY"

In Order to Renounce Sin and Embrace Holiness

you must... "Choose Wisely"

Joshua 24:14-15

As illustrated in Joshua 24:14-15, making wise choices is fundamental in the journey of renouncing sin and embracing holiness. The decisions we make daily shape our character and influence our spiritual path. When we choose wisely, we align ourselves with values that promote righteousness and integrity, steering clear of temptations that lead to sin.

Firstly, wise choices involve discernment. This means evaluating situations and understanding the potential consequences of our actions. By cultivating a habit of reflection, we can better recognize the allure of sinful behavior and the fleeting satisfaction it may offer. Instead, we can focus on choices that foster spiritual growth and align with our commitment to holiness.

Moreover, choosing wisely often requires surrounding ourselves with positive influences. The company we keep plays a significant role in our decision-making process. Engaging with individuals who share our values and aspirations can inspire us to make choices that reflect our desire for holiness. These relationships can provide accountability and encouragement, helping us to resist the pull of sin.

Additionally, wise decision-making is rooted in knowledge and understanding. By immersing ourselves in spiritual teachings and Scriptures, we gain insight into what it means to live a holy life. This knowledge empowers us to make informed choices that reflect our commitment to righteousness. When we understand the principles of holiness, we are better equipped to reject sinful temptations.

Finally, embracing a mindset of prayer and reflection can guide us in our decision-making. Seeking divine guidance allows us to align our choices with a higher purpose. Through prayer, we can ask for strength to resist sin and the wisdom to choose paths that lead to holiness.

In conclusion, the act of choosing wisely is a powerful tool in the pursuit of a holy life. By exercising discernment, surrounding ourselves with positive influences, seeking knowledge, and engaging in prayer, we can effectively renounce sin and embrace a life of holiness. Each choice we make is a step toward a more fulfilling and spiritually enriched existence.

In Order to Renounce Sin and Embrace Holiness

you must... "Choose Wisely"

Here's an example...

A biblical character who chose wisely is King Solomon, especially in the story of his request for wisdom in 1 Kings 3. When Solomon ascended the throne of Israel after his father, King David, died, he was a young and inexperienced ruler. In a dream, God appeared to Solomon and offered to grant him anything he desired. Instead of asking for wealth, long life, or the death of his enemies, Solomon humbly asked for wisdom to govern God's people well, saying, "Give your servant a discerning heart to govern your people and to distinguish between right and wrong" (1 Kings 3:9).

God was pleased with Solomon's selfless request and granted him wisdom greater than anyone before or after him, along with wealth and honor. Solomon's wisdom became renowned across the ancient world, attracting visitors like the Queen of Sheba (1 Kings 10). One of the most famous examples of his wisdom is his judgment in the case of two women who claimed to be the mother of the same baby. Solomon proposed to divide the child in two, but the real mother immediately offered to give up her claim to save the child, revealing her identity.

Solomon's choice to seek wisdom over worldly desires shows a heart that values understanding and discernment in decision-making, making him a model of wise leadership.

Here's some practical steps...

- Understand the importance of seeking God's guidance in decision-making.
- Pray for wisdom and discernment before making choices.
- Study relevant Scripture passages that address decision-making.
- Consider the counsel of wise and godly individuals in your community.
- Reflect on the potential consequences of your choices.
- Align your decisions with biblical principles and values.
- Evaluate your motivations and intentions behind each choice.
- Trust in God's plan and timing for your life.
- Be open to the leading of the Holy Spirit in your decisions.
- Commit your plans to the Lord and seek His approval.

Journal Your Thoughts

In Order to Renounce Sin and Embrace Holiness

10

You Must...

"DEPEND ON GOD"

In Order to Renounce Sin and Embrace Holiness
you must... "Depend on God"
Proverbs 3:5-6

Relying on God enables individuals to reject sin and wholeheartedly adopt a life of holiness. When we place our trust in God, we invite His strength and guidance into our lives, which is essential for overcoming the temptations that lead us astray. As seen in Proverbs 3:5-6, this dependence fosters a deep relationship with the Creator, allowing us to draw upon His wisdom and love, which are crucial in our pursuit of righteousness.

As we cultivate our faith, we begin to understand the nature of sin and its consequences. God's teachings illuminate the path to holiness, revealing the beauty of living in alignment with His will. This understanding encourages us to renounce sinful behaviors that once seemed appealing. The more we immerse ourselves in God's Word and prayer, the more we develop a desire to reflect His character in our lives.

Depending on God fosters a strong sense of duty. When we acknowledge that our strength comes from Him, we are less likely to succumb to the pressures of the world. We learn to seek His help in moments of weakness, allowing His grace to empower us to make better choices. This reliance fosters resilience, enabling us to resist temptation and pursue a life that honors God.

Additionally, embracing holiness becomes a natural outcome of our relationship with God. As we grow closer to Him, we begin to mirror His attributes, such as love, kindness, and integrity. This transformation not only impacts our personal lives but also influences those around us, as we become beacons of light in a world often shrouded in darkness.

In conclusion, depending on God is essential for renouncing sin and embracing holiness. It is through this reliance that we find the strength to overcome our shortcomings and the motivation to live a life that reflects His glory.

IN ORDER TO RENOUNCE SIN AND EMBRACE HOLINESS
YOU MUST... "DEPEND ON GOD"

Here's an example...

One biblical character who demonstrated complete dependence on God was the prophet Elijah. In a time when Israel had turned to idolatry and the worship of Baal, Elijah boldly proclaimed God's sovereignty and His power over all things. His life was marked by moments where he had to trust God fully, often in circumstances of extreme danger or isolation.

In 1 Kings 17, during a severe drought, God directed Elijah to go to a widow in Zarephath, promising that her jar of flour and jug of oil would never run out. Despite the widow's initial doubts, she obeyed God's command through Elijah, and their resources were miraculously sustained. Elijah's dependence on God was also evident during the showdown with the prophets of Baal on Mount Carmel (1 Kings 18). When all seemed hopeless, Elijah placed complete trust in God to send fire from heaven to prove His power, and God answered in dramatic fashion.

Elijah's life is a testament to unwavering faith in God's provision, protection, and power. In times of physical danger, emotional distress, and uncertainty, Elijah's reliance on God never wavered, demonstrating a life fully surrendered to God's will and purpose. Through Elijah, we see that trust in God brings victory even in the most impossible circumstances.

Here's some practical steps...

- Understand the importance of faith in God as outlined in Scripture.
- Study biblical passages that emphasize reliance on God's promises.
- Pray regularly to strengthen your relationship with God.
- Seek guidance from the Holy Spirit in decision-making.
- Trust in God's plan, even when circumstances are challenging.
- Reflect on personal experiences of God's faithfulness in your life.
- Engage with a community of believers for support and encouragement.
- Meditate on God's Word to deepen your understanding of His character.
- Acknowledge your limitations and surrender control to God.
- Cultivate a heart of gratitude for God's provision and care.

Journal Your Thoughts

IN ORDER TO RENOUNCE SIN AND EMBRACE HOLINESS

11

You Must...

"HEED TO WHAT IS RIGHT"

In Order to Renounce Sin and Embrace Holiness
you must... "Heed to What is Right"
Proverbs 16:20

Choosing to do what is right is a powerful step toward renouncing sin and embracing a life of holiness. When we consciously decide to act in accordance with our values and moral principles, we create a pathway that leads us away from temptation and toward a more virtuous existence (Proverbs 16:20). This journey begins with self-awareness and a commitment to integrity, allowing us to recognize the choices that align with our higher selves.

Engaging in righteous actions fosters a sense of inner peace and fulfillment. Each time we choose kindness over cruelty, honesty over deceit, or compassion over indifference, we reinforce our commitment to a life of holiness. These choices not only uplift our spirits but also inspire those around us, creating a ripple effect of positivity and moral courage in our communities.

Moreover, the act of doing what is right serves as a shield against the allure of sin. When we fill our lives with good deeds and positive intentions, we find it easier to resist the temptations that lead us astray. The more we practice righteousness, the more it becomes ingrained in our character, transforming our desires and priorities. This transformation is essential for anyone seeking to live a life that reflects their deepest values.

Embracing holiness goes beyond simply steering clear of mistakes; it is about actively pursuing a life that reflects love, justice, and truth. By committing ourselves to righteous actions, we cultivate a deeper relationship with our spiritual beliefs and a clearer understanding of our purpose. This journey is not always easy, but it is profoundly rewarding. As we strive to do what is right, we not only renounce sin but also open ourselves to the beauty and grace that holiness brings into our lives.

In Order to Renounce Sin and Embrace Holiness
you must... "Heed to What is Right"

Here's an example...

One biblical character who lived righteously before God is Noah. In a time when the world was filled with corruption and wickedness, Noah stood out as a man who walked faithfully with God. The book of Genesis describes Noah as "a righteous man, blameless among the people of his time" (Genesis 6:9). God saw Noah's integrity in the midst of a sinful generation, and it was for this reason that God chose him to build the ark and preserve life during the coming flood.

Noah's righteousness was demonstrated in his obedience to God's commands, even when they seemed difficult or strange. When God instructed Noah to build an enormous ark to survive a coming deluge, Noah did not hesitate, despite the ridicule he likely faced from his peers. He trusted God's Word and acted on it, gathering the animals and preparing the ark as directed (Genesis 6:22).

Furthermore, after the flood, Noah continued to honor God by offering sacrifices and living in obedience to His will. His life shows the importance of unwavering faith and obedience, even when it goes against the norms of society. Noah's righteousness led to his family's salvation, and he remains an enduring example of faithfulness in a fallen world.

Here's some practical steps...

- Explore the principles of righteous living as outlined in the Holy Bible.
- Understand the importance of faith and trust in God for a righteous life.
- Study the teachings of Jesus Christ and their application in daily life.
- Embrace the values of love, compassion, and forgiveness.
- Follow the commandments and guidelines provided in Scripture.
- Engage in regular prayer to strengthen your relationship with God.
- Participate in church to support and encourage righteous behavior.
- Reflect on personal actions and decisions in light of biblical teachings.
- Seek wisdom from biblical figures and their examples of righteous living.
- Commit to continuous growth and learning in your spiritual journey.

Journal Your Thoughts

In Order to Renounce Sin and Embrace Holiness

12

You Must...

"AVOID LETTING PRAISE DISTRACT"

In Order to Renounce Sin and Embrace Holiness

you must... "Avoid Letting Praise Distract"
Matthew 21:12

Avoiding the distraction of praise is crucial for anyone seeking to renounce sin and embrace holiness. After Jesus entered Jerusalem, welcomed by the cheers and admiration of the crowd, He remained resolute in addressing the corruption and mismanagement within the temple. The adoration of the people did not sway His discernment regarding God's intentions (Matthew 21:12). When we receive accolades or compliments, it can be easy to become complacent or even prideful. This distraction can lead us away from our spiritual goals and the pursuit of a righteous life. Instead of focusing on our relationship with God and the principles of holiness, we may find ourselves preoccupied with how others perceive us.

By consciously choosing to set aside the allure of praise, we create space for genuine self-reflection and growth. This allows us to examine our actions and intentions more critically. When we are not seeking validation from others, we can better align our lives with our values and beliefs. This alignment is essential for renouncing sin, as it encourages us to confront our shortcomings without the noise of external approval.

Moreover, avoiding the distraction of praise helps cultivate humility. Humility is a foundational aspect of holiness, as it reminds us that our worth is not determined by human accolades but by our relationship with God. When we embrace humility, we become more receptive to guidance and correction, which are vital for spiritual growth. This openness allows us to recognize and address sinful behaviors more effectively.

Additionally, focusing on our spiritual journey rather than external validation fosters a deeper connection with God. When we prioritize our relationship with Him, we are more likely to seek His will and guidance in our lives. This pursuit of divine connection empowers us to resist temptation and make choices that reflect our commitment to holiness.

In conclusion, steering clear of the distractions that come with praise enables us to focus on our spiritual development. By renouncing the need for external validation, we can cultivate humility, deepen our relationship with God, and ultimately embrace a life of holiness. This intentional approach not only strengthens our resolve against sin but also enriches our spiritual journey.

IN ORDER TO RENOUNCE SIN AND EMBRACE HOLINESS
YOU MUST... "AVOID LETTING PRAISE DISTRACT"

Here's an example...

A biblical character who exemplified not allowing the praise of men to distract from the will of God is the prophet Jeremiah. Throughout his ministry, Jeremiah faced intense opposition and criticism from his contemporaries, yet he remained steadfast in proclaiming God's message, regardless of how it was received.

In Jeremiah 1, God called him to be a prophet to the nations, but Jeremiah was initially reluctant, feeling inadequate. However, God assured him that He would be with him and would give him the words to speak (Jeremiah 1:7-9). As Jeremiah faithfully delivered God's warnings and messages, he encountered rejection, mockery, and persecution.

Despite the resistance, Jeremiah did not seek the approval of men. In Jeremiah 15:10, he laments his situation but is clear that his commitment to God's calling surpasses any desire for human praise.

Jeremiah's refusal to compromise the truth, even when it meant rejection and scorn, shows a life dedicated to obeying God's will over the fleeting approval of people. His story is a powerful reminder of the cost of faithfulness and the importance of prioritizing God's approval above all.

Here's some practical steps...

- Focus on God's approval rather than seeking validation from others.
- Remember that human praise is temporary and can lead to pride.
- Examine cases of people who placed God's will above human desires.
- Engage in regular prayer to seek guidance and strength against distractions.
- Meditate on Scripture that emphasizes humility and servitude.
- Associate with people that value spiritual growth over worldly recognition.
- Reflect on the teachings of Jesus about the dangers of seeking human praise.
- Celebrate and worship God instead of seeking accolades from people.
- Set your goals to align with biblical values rather than societal expectations.
- Continuously evaluate your motivations and intentions in your behavior.

Journal Your Thoughts

In Order to Renounce Sin and Embrace Holiness

13

You Must...

"NEVER FORGET GOD"

In Order to Renounce Sin and Embrace Holiness

you must... "Never Forget God"
Psalm 103:17

Remembering God in our daily lives serves as a powerful anchor that can guide us away from sin and toward a life of holiness. When we keep God at the forefront of our thoughts, we cultivate a deeper awareness of His presence and His expectations for us. This awareness acts as a moral compass, steering us away from temptations that lead to sinful behavior (Psalm 103:17).

By consistently reflecting on God's teachings and His love for us, we develop a stronger desire to align our actions with His will. This relationship encourages a feeling of responsibility; we recognize that our choices not only affect us but also our relationship with God. When we truly understand the depth of His grace and mercy, we are inspired to live in a way that honors Him, which naturally leads us to renounce sin.

Moreover, remembering God encourages us to seek His guidance in moments of weakness. When faced with temptation, recalling His promises and the joy of living a holy life can empower us to make better choices. Prayer and meditation on Scripture become vital tools in this process, allowing us to draw strength from our faith. The more we immerse ourselves in God's Word, the more we are equipped to resist the allure of sin.

Embracing holiness is not merely about avoiding wrongdoing; it's about actively pursuing a life that reflects God's character. When we remember God, we are reminded of His call to love, kindness, and integrity. This pursuit of holiness transforms our hearts and minds, enabling us to see the beauty in living a life that is pleasing to Him.

In essence, never forgetting God is a commitment to a relationship that shapes our identity and influences our choices. It empowers us to reject sin and embrace a life filled with purpose, joy, and fulfillment in His presence. By keeping God close, we find the strength to live righteously and experience the profound peace that comes from walking in His light.

IN ORDER TO RENOUNCE SIN AND EMBRACE HOLINESS
YOU MUST... "NEVER FORGET GOD"

Here's an example...

A biblical character who never forgot God and His commands is Simeon, a devout man mentioned in the Gospel of Luke. Simeon is described as "righteous and devout," waiting for the consolation of Israel, which refers to the coming of the Messiah (Luke 2:25). He lived with a deep sense of anticipation and faith in God's promises, demonstrating his unwavering devotion to God throughout his life.

Simeon had been promised by the Holy Spirit that he would not die before seeing the Messiah, and he remained faithful to that promise, never losing hope or forgetting God's Word. When Mary and Joseph brought the infant Jesus to the temple, Simeon, led by the Holy Spirit, recognized Jesus as the promised Savior. He then joyfully proclaimed that he had seen God's salvation, saying, "Sovereign Lord, as you have promised, you may now dismiss your servant in peace" (Luke 2:29).

Simeon's life exemplifies a continual remembrance of God's promises and His commands. He lived in eager expectation of God's fulfillment of the prophecies and remained steadfast in his faith until he saw the culmination of God's plan. Simeon's story highlights the importance of faithfully holding onto God's Word, trusting that He will fulfill His promises in His perfect timing.

Here's some practical steps...

- Regularly read and study the Bible to understand God's teachings.
- Pray daily to maintain a close relationship with God.
- Memorize key verses that remind you of God's presence.
- Attend church services to stay connected with the faith community.
- Reflect on God's blessings and goodness in your life.
- Keep a journal of your spiritual journey and experiences with God.
- Share your faith with others to reinforce your beliefs.
- Set reminders for spiritual practices throughout your day.
- Engage in worship and praise to honor God regularly.
- Seek guidance from spiritual leaders or mentors for support.

Journal Your Thoughts

In Order to Renounce Sin and Embrace Holiness

14

You Must...

"BE IN CHRIST"

In Order to Renounce Sin and Embrace Holiness
you must... "Be in Christ"
John 15:4-8

Being in a relationship with Christ is a life-changing experience that provides immense support as we strive to turn away from sin and pursue holiness. When we align ourselves with Him, we access a divine reservoir of strength and wisdom that helps us navigate the challenges and temptations we face. This connection goes beyond mere rule-following; it's about nurturing a profound, personal bond with the Savior who knows our vulnerabilities and is eager to assist us in our growth.

At its core, being in Christ means we are embraced by His grace. This grace is not a one-off event; it is a continuous stream of love and forgiveness that inspires us to abandon our sinful ways. When we truly understand the magnitude of Christ's sacrifice and the depth of His love for us, we feel compelled to live in a manner that honors Him (2 Cor. 5:14). This realization ignites a desire to reject sin, as we become aware that our choices can either bring us closer to Him or create barriers in our relationship.

Furthermore, being in Christ grants us the Holy Spirit, who serves as our guide and advisor. The Spirit brings conviction regarding our sins, illuminating the areas in our lives that require transformation. This internal guidance is vital; it not only points out our flaws but also empowers us to make meaningful changes. With the Spirit's assistance, we can cultivate new habits that embody holiness, replacing old behaviors with actions that resonate with God's will.

Additionally, being part of a community of believers fortifies our commitment. Engaging with others who share our dedication to Christ fosters accountability and encouragement. Together, we can support one another, share our challenges, and celebrate our successes in the journey toward holiness.

In summary, being in a relationship with Christ is crucial for anyone wishing to turn away from sin and embrace a holy life (John 15:4-8). Through His grace, the guidance of the Holy Spirit, and the encouragement of a faith community, we are empowered to fulfill our calling as children of God, shining His light in the world.

In Order to Renounce Sin and Embrace Holiness

you must... "Be in Christ"

Here's an example...

A biblical character who lived their life "in Christ" is Philip the Evangelist. Philip is an example of someone who faithfully followed Christ's commission to spread the Gospel and live out his faith, even in difficult circumstances.

Philip's life in Christ is evident in his boldness in evangelism and his obedience to the Holy Spirit. In Acts 8, when persecution scattered the early church, Philip traveled to Samaria and preached the Gospel with great success, performing miracles and baptizing many (Acts 8:4-13). His ministry was so effective that it brought great joy to the city.

Later, Philip is led by the Spirit to encounter the Ethiopian eunuch, a man seeking to understand Scripture (Acts 8:26-40). Philip explains the Gospel to him, and the eunuch is baptized. This moment highlights Philip's commitment to obeying God's call, regardless of the situation, and his willingness to serve as an instrument for others to come to faith in Christ.

Philip's life demonstrates living "in Christ" through faithful service, listening to the Holy Spirit, and being willing to share the message of salvation with others. His legacy as an evangelist shows the transformative power of living out the Gospel in everyday life.

Here's some practical steps...

- Understand the teachings of Jesus in the New Testament.
- Read and study the Bible regularly for guidance.
- Pray daily to strengthen your relationship with God.
- Follow the commandments and teachings found in Scripture.
- Show love and kindness to others as Jesus taught.
- Attend church services for community and support.
- Share your faith and the message of Christ with others.
- Practice forgiveness and seek reconciliation with those around you.
- Live with integrity and honesty in all your actions.
- Trust in God's plan and seek His will in your life.

Journal Your Thoughts

In Order to Renounce Sin and Embrace Holiness

15

You Must...

"CIRCUMVENT SADNESS"

In Order to Renounce Sin and Embrace Holiness

you must... "Circumvent Sadness"

Philippians 4:8

Overcoming sadness can be a powerful journey that fosters a stronger dedication to rejecting sin and embracing a life of holiness. When we allow ourselves to linger in sadness, it becomes challenging to rise above our situations and make decisions that resonate with our core values. Sadness can obscure our judgment, making it easier to give in to temptations and engage in actions that divert us from our spiritual path. By consciously striving to overcome sadness, we open the door to joy, hope, and clarity—essential elements for a holy life.

Choosing positivity and engaging in uplifting activities can dramatically transform our mindset (Philippians 4:8). By concentrating on the positive aspects of our lives, we nurture gratitude and appreciation, which act as potent remedies for despair. This change in outlook not only boosts our emotional health but also fortifies our determination to turn away from sinful actions. When we are filled with joy and a sense of purpose, we are less inclined to partake in behaviors that contradict our values.

Additionally, surrounding ourselves with encouraging communities and participating in spiritual practices can further assist us in navigating through sadness. These relationships offer support and accountability, reminding us of our commitment to holiness. By prioritizing our spiritual development and striving to uplift ourselves and those around us, we cultivate an environment that promotes righteousness and deters sin.

Ultimately, overcoming sadness is not just about evading negative feelings; it is about making a conscious choice to pursue a path that brings us closer to holiness. By emphasizing joy, gratitude, and community, we empower ourselves to make decisions that align with our deepest values. This proactive mindset not only aids us in renouncing sin but also enriches our spiritual journey, enabling us to lead a life that is genuinely fulfilling and in harmony with our highest goals.

In Order to Renounce Sin and Embrace Holiness

you must... "Circumvent Sadness"

Here's an example...

One biblical character who exemplifies overcoming sadness is King David. Throughout his life, David experienced profound emotional lows, including periods of deep despair, betrayal, and personal failure. Yet, he consistently turned to God for solace and strength, illustrating a profound resilience in the face of hardship.

In the Psalms, many of which were written by David, we find raw expressions of sorrow, lament, and mourning. For example, in Psalm 42, David asks, "Why are you cast down, O my soul? Why so disturbed within me?" (Psalm 42:5, NIV), yet he encourages himself by saying, "Put your hope in God, for I will yet praise him, my Savior and my God." Through this, David teaches us that sadness and despair are natural human experiences, but they need not define us. By focusing on God's faithfulness and maintaining hope, David found the strength to move beyond his sadness.

David's life was not without suffering—he faced the loss of his child (2 Samuel 12:15-23), the rebellion of his son Absalom (2 Samuel 15), and countless battles. Yet through it all, he remained steadfast in his faith, proving that with God's help, even in our darkest moments, we can find the courage to persevere and rise above sadness.

Here's some practical steps...

- Explore biblical teachings on joy and hope as antidotes to sadness.
- Reflect on Psalms for comfort and reassurance during difficult times.
- Engage in prayer to seek divine guidance and peace.
- Practice gratitude by acknowledging blessings in your life.
- Surround yourself with a supportive community of believers.
- Meditate on Scripture that emphasizes God's love and faithfulness.
- Participate in worship to uplift your spirit and connect with God.
- Serve others to find purpose and fulfillment beyond personal struggles.
- Embrace the promise of eternal life as a source of enduring joy.
- Seek counsel from spiritual leaders for wisdom and encouragement.

Journal Your Thoughts

In Order to Renounce Sin and Embrace Holiness

16

You Must...

"RESPOND APPROPRIATELY"

In Order to Renounce Sin and Embrace Holiness

you must... "Respond Appropriately"
Psalm 116:1-14

Acknowledging God's goodness can greatly support the process of turning away from sin and welcoming a life of holiness. When we recognize the depth of God's love and grace in our lives, it ignites a profound sense of gratitude and reverence within us (Psalm 116:1-14). This awareness compels us to reflect on our actions and choices, prompting us to seek a life that aligns more closely with biblical principles.

Understanding God's goodness encourages us to cultivate a heart of thankfulness. When we acknowledge the blessings we receive, we become more aware of the contrast between our lives and the holiness that God embodies. This realization can lead to a desire to turn away from sinful behaviors that distance us from Him. Instead of viewing holiness as a set of restrictive rules, we begin to see it as a pathway to a more fulfilling and joyful life, one that is enriched by our relationship with God.

Moreover, responding to God's goodness fosters a deeper connection with Him. As we engage in prayer, worship, and the study of Scripture, we become more attuned to His will for our lives. This spiritual intimacy empowers us to resist temptation and make choices that reflect our commitment to holiness. The more we experience God's goodness, the more we are inspired to live in a way that honors Him, leading us to renounce sin and pursue righteousness.

Additionally, embracing God's goodness can transform our perspective on sin itself. Instead of viewing it as a mere list of do's and don'ts, we start to see sin as a barrier that hinders our relationship with God. This shift in perspective motivates us to let go of behaviors that do not serve our spiritual growth.

Ultimately, responding to God's goodness is not just about avoiding sin; it is about actively choosing to live in a way that reflects His love and grace, allowing us to fully embrace the holiness He desires for us.

In Order to Renounce Sin and Embrace Holiness
you must... "Respond Appropriately"

Here's an example...

In Luke 17:11-19, the story of the ten lepers vividly demonstrates how one individual responded appropriately to God's goodness. Ten lepers, all desperate for healing, cried out to Jesus for mercy as He passed by. Jesus, moved with compassion, instructed them to show themselves to the priests. As they obeyed, all were miraculously healed. However, only one—a Samaritan—returned to thank Jesus, falling at His feet in worship.

This Samaritan leper exemplifies the proper response to God's grace. While the other nine were content with their physical healing and continued on their way, the Samaritan recognized the deeper significance of his healing: it was an act of divine mercy. Instead of just being satisfied with the blessing, he returned to express his gratitude, understanding that the healing was not just a physical restoration, but a moment of spiritual encounter with God.

Jesus commended the Samaritan, saying, "Your faith has made you well." His response was not just one of gratitude but also of faith, acknowledging Jesus as the source of his healing. In returning to Jesus, he demonstrated a heart of thankfulness and reverence, which is the appropriate way to respond to God's goodness—by recognizing His power and grace and offering our worship in return.

Here's some practical steps...

- Explore the biblical principles for acknowledging God's goodness.
- Reflect on Scripture that highlights God's benevolence and mercy.
- Discuss the importance of gratitude in responding to God's blessings.
- Examine how prayer can be a means of expressing appreciation.
- Consider the role of worship in recognizing and celebrating God's nature.
- Study the significance of sharing testimonies of God's goodness.
- Investigate how acts of kindness can be a response to God's generosity.
- Look into the concept of stewardship as a way to honor God's gifts.
- Encourage a lifestyle of obedience as a response to God's goodness.
- Highlight the importance of community praise acknowledging God's grace.

Journal Your Thoughts

In Order to Renounce Sin and Embrace Holiness

17

You Must...

"BE DETERMINED TO SUCCEED"

In Order to Renounce Sin and Embrace Holiness

you must... "Be Determined to Succeed"
Psalm 101

Determination to succeed functions as a significant motivator for personal transformation, especially when it comes to renouncing sin and embracing holiness. When you set your sights on a goal, particularly one that aligns with moral and spiritual values, you cultivate a mindset that prioritizes growth and integrity. The psalmist in Psalm 101 consistently expressed his eagerness to serve God, showcasing a strong resolve to achieve his goals. This unwavering commitment to success can serve as a guiding light, illumi-nating the path away from temptation and towards a life of virtue.

First and foremost, determination fosters resilience. Life is filled with challenges and distractions that can lead one astray. However, when you are resolute in your desire to succeed, you develop the strength to resist these temptations. Each time you face a moral dilemma, your determination acts as a shield, empowering you to make choices that reflect your commitment to holiness. This resilience not only helps you avoid sin but also reinforces your character, making it easier to choose righteousness in the future.

Moreover, a determined mindset encourages self-discipline. Success often requires hard work, focus, and the ability to delay gratification. By honing these skills, you naturally cultivate a lifestyle that is less conducive to sinful behavior. The more you practice self-control in pursuit of your goals, the more it becomes ingrained in your daily life. This discipline translates into your spiritual journey, allowing you to prioritize your relationship with God and engage in practices that foster holiness.

Additionally, determination can inspire a sense of purpose. When you are driven by a clear vision of success, you are more likely to seek out positive influences and surround yourself with individuals who share your values. This supportive community can provide encouragement and accountability, further reinforcing your commitment to renounce sin.

In conclusion, being determined to succeed is not just about achieving personal goals; it is a transformative force that can lead you away from sin and towards a life of holiness. Embrace this determination, and watch as it shapes your character and guides your choices toward a more virtuous existence.

IN ORDER TO RENOUNCE SIN AND EMBRACE HOLINESS
YOU MUST... "BE DETERMINED TO SUCCEED"

Here's an example...

One biblical character who exemplifies determination and perseverance is Ruth. Ruth's story is told in the Book of Ruth, and her life is a powerful example of loyalty, faith, and resilience. Ruth was a Moabite widow who chose to stay with her mother-in-law, Naomi, after both of their husbands died. Despite the cultural norms and the hardships of being a foreigner in Israel, Ruth made a firm decision to follow Naomi back to Bethlehem.

Ruth's determination to succeed was rooted in her unwavering commitment to Naomi and to the God of Israel. When Naomi urged her to return to her own people, Ruth refused, famously declaring, "Where you go, I will go; where you stay, I will stay. Your people will be my people, and your God my God" (Ruth 1:16). This statement was more than just a pledge of loyalty—it was a declaration of faith and trust in God's provision.

Ruth's dedication led her to glean in the fields of Boaz, a relative of Naomi's, and eventually, through God's providence, she married Boaz, securing both her future and Naomi's. Ruth's perseverance and faithfulness not only ensured her success but also placed her in the lineage of King David, and ultimately, the lineage of Jesus Christ.

Here's some practical steps...

- Understand the importance of faith in achieving success.
- Embrace perseverance, and its ultimate benefit, found in James 1:12.
- Set clear goals that align with biblical principles and values.
- Seek wisdom through prayer and meditation on the Word of God.
- Cultivate a strong work ethic that reflects biblical diligence.
- Surround yourself with supportive and like-minded individuals.
- Trust in God's plan and timing, even when faced with obstacles.
- Learn from failures and setbacks, viewing them as opportunities for growth.
- Practice gratitude, recognizing that success is a blessing from God.
- Commit to continuous learning and improvement.

Journal Your Thoughts

IN ORDER TO RENOUNCE SIN AND EMBRACE HOLINESS

18

You Must...

"GIVE WHOLEHEARTEDLY"

In Order to Renounce Sin and Embrace Holiness
you must... "Give Wholeheartedly"
2 Corinthians 9

According to 2 Corinthians 9, embracing a life of selflessness can profoundly influence one's journey towards renouncing sin and cultivating holiness. When individuals commit to giving of themselves wholeheartedly, they create a transformative environment that fosters spiritual growth and moral integrity. This act of self-giving is not merely a gesture; it is a deep-seated commitment to living in alignment with higher values and principles.

Firstly, the act of giving oneself to others encourages a shift in focus from self-centered desires to the needs of those around us. This shift is crucial in overcoming sinful tendencies, as it redirects attention away from personal gratification and towards acts of kindness and compassion. By engaging in selfless acts, individuals often find that their own struggles with sin diminish, as they become more attuned to the well-being of others. This connection fosters a sense of community and accountability, which can further reinforce one's commitment to living a holy life.

Moreover, giving of oneself can lead to a deeper understanding of one's own values and beliefs. As individuals engage in acts of service, they often reflect on their motivations and the impact of their actions. This introspection can illuminate areas of life that may require change, prompting a sincere desire to renounce behaviors that do not align with a holy lifestyle. The process of self-examination, spurred by acts of giving, can lead to profound personal transformation.

Additionally, the practice of self-giving cultivates virtues such as humility, patience, and love. These qualities are essential in the pursuit of holiness, as they enable individuals to respond to challenges with grace and understanding. By embodying these virtues, one not only enhances their own spiritual journey but also inspires others to seek a similar path.

In conclusion, wholeheartedly giving of oneself serves as a powerful catalyst for renouncing sin and embracing holiness. Through selfless acts, individuals can foster a deeper connection with others, gain clarity on their values, and cultivate essential virtues, all of which contribute to a more meaningful and holy life.

IN ORDER TO RENOUNCE SIN AND EMBRACE HOLINESS
YOU MUST... "GIVE WHOLEHEARTEDLY"

Here's an example...

The Berean church, as described in Acts 17:10-12, offers a powerful example of giving wholeheartedly, not just in material ways, but in their devotion to truth and spiritual growth. When Paul and Silas arrived in Berea, they preached the gospel, and the Bereans responded with eagerness and an open heart. The Bible says, "Now the Bereans were of more noble character than the Thessalonians, for they received the message with great eagerness and examined the Scriptures every day to see if what Paul said was true" (Acts 17:11).

The Bereans exemplified wholeheartedness by giving their time, attention, and effort to the Word of God. They didn't merely accept what Paul said at face value; instead, they searched the Scriptures daily to verify the truth of his message. This diligent and sincere pursuit of knowledge reflected a deep commitment to understanding and living out God's will.

Their wholehearted devotion to the gospel is a reminder of how we, too, should give ourselves entirely to seeking God's truth, allowing it to shape our lives. Just as the Bereans gave their minds and hearts to the study of Scripture, we are called to give our whole selves—our time, attention, and resources—to God's work and truth.

Here's some practical steps...

- Understand the principle of giving as outlined in the Bible.
- Recognize that giving should come from a place of love and generosity.
- Reflect on 2 Corinthians 9:7, which emphasizes cheerful giving.
- Acknowledge that God loves a giver who is willing and eager.
- Consider the importance of giving without expecting anything in return.
- Explore the concept of tithing as a biblical standard for giving.
- Remember that giving should be a personal decision, not coerced.
- Seek to support those in need as an expression of faith and compassion.
- Pray for guidance on how to give effectively and meaningfully.
- Trust that God will provide for your needs as you give to others.

Journal Your Thoughts

In Order to Renounce Sin and Embrace Holiness

19

You Must...

"WALK WORTHY OF YOUR CALLING"

In Order to Renounce Sin and Embrace Holiness

you must... "Walk Worthy of Your Calling"
Ephesians 4:1

Embracing a life that reflects your calling is a profound journey that enables you to turn away from sin and welcome holiness. When you grasp the importance of your calling, it serves as a beacon, lighting your way toward righteousness. This realization fosters a deep sense of purpose, inspiring you to align your actions with your core values and beliefs.

As you endeavor to live in a way that honors your calling, you start to see how your choices shape your life. Every decision becomes a testament to your dedication to a higher ideal. This heightened awareness allows you to pinpoint behaviors and habits that might divert you from a holy path. By consciously choosing to reject sin, you open the door to spiritual growth and renewal.

Embracing holiness goes beyond merely steering clear of wrongdoing; it involves nurturing a life that exudes goodness and virtue. When you walk in alignment with your calling, you invite the divine presence of the Lord into your everyday existence. This connection fortifies your determination to resist temptation and ignites a desire to live in harmony with God's will. You become more sensitive to the gentle nudges of your conscience, guiding you toward actions that embody love, compassion, and integrity.

Additionally, living in accordance with your calling cultivates a sense of community and accountability. Being surrounded by individuals who share your commitment to holiness can offer invaluable encouragement and support. Together, you can uplift one another, exchange experiences, and hold each other accountable on your shared journey. This collective effort strengthens your resolve to reject sin and pursue a life that honors your calling.

Ultimately, walking in a manner worthy of your calling represents a comprehensive approach to living with purpose and integrity (Ephesians 4:1). It empowers you to turn away from sin and embrace holiness, transforming not just your life but also the lives of those around you. As you progress on this path, you will discover that each step taken in faith brings you closer to realizing your divine purpose.

In Order to Renounce Sin and Embrace Holiness
You must... "Walk Worthy of Your Calling"

Here's an example...

One biblical character who faithfully operated according to his calling is Gideon, as recorded in the Book of Judges, chapters 6–8. Gideon was called by God to deliver the Israelites from the oppressive rule of the Midianites. Initially, he was reluctant and unsure of his ability, saying, "Pardon me, my lord, but how can I save Israel? My clan is the weakest in Manasseh, and I am the least in my family" (Judges 6:15). Despite his doubts, God assured him of His presence and strength.

Gideon's calling required him to rise up in faith, even when faced with seemingly insurmountable odds. God instructed him to reduce his army from 32,000 men to just 300, demonstrating that the victory would be by God's power, not human strength. Gideon followed God's instructions, leading his small, faithful army to victory against the Midianites in a miraculous way.

Gideon's story highlights the importance of obedience to God's call, even when it seems impossible or when we feel inadequate. Though he initially hesitated, Gideon ultimately stepped out in faith, and his obedience to God's direction resulted in the liberation of Israel. His story is a reminder that God equips those He calls and empowers them to fulfill their purpose.

Here's some practical steps...

- Understand your unique calling as outlined in Scripture.
- Seek guidance through prayer and meditation on biblical texts.
- Identify your spiritual gifts and how they align with your calling.
- Study the lives of biblical figures who exemplified their callings.
- Engage in community and fellowship to discern your purpose.
- Embrace opportunities for service that reflect your calling.
- Remain open to the Holy Spirit's leading in your decisions.
- Cultivate a lifestyle of obedience to God's Word.
- Share your journey and insights with others for encouragement.
- Trust in God's timing and provision as you fulfill your calling.

Journal Your Thoughts

In Order to Renounce Sin and Embrace Holiness

20

You Must...

"WALK DIFFERENTLY"

In Order to Renounce Sin and Embrace Holiness

you must... "Walk Differently"

Ephesians 4:17-24

Walking in accordance with biblical principles can profoundly influence our ability to renounce sin and embrace holiness. The Bible often uses the metaphor of walking to describe our daily choices and the path we choose in life. When we align our walk with the teachings of Scripture, we create a foundation for a life that reflects God's holiness (Ephesians 4:17-24).

Firstly, walking differently means adopting a mindset that prioritizes spiritual growth over worldly desires. Romans 12:2 encourages us not to conform to the patterns of this world but to be transformed by the renewing of our minds. This transformation begins with a conscious decision to seek God's will in every aspect of our lives. By immersing ourselves in the Word, we gain insight into what it means to live righteously, allowing us to identify and reject sinful behaviors that may have previously gone unchecked.

Moreover, walking in the Spirit, as described in Galatians 5:16, empowers us to resist temptation. When we cultivate a relationship with the Holy Spirit, we receive guidance and strength to make choices that align with God's desires. This divine support helps us to turn away from sin and pursue a life characterized by love, joy, peace, and self-control. As we practice walking in the Spirit, we become more attuned to the subtle ways sin can creep into our lives, enabling us to take proactive steps to avoid it.

Additionally, embracing holiness requires accountability and community. Hebrews 10:24-25 emphasizes the importance of encouraging one another in our faith journeys. By surrounding ourselves with fellow believers who share our commitment to walking in a manner worthy of our calling, we create an environment that fosters growth and accountability. This support system can help us stay focused on our goal of holiness, reminding us of the importance of renouncing sin.

In conclusion, adopting a different approach to walking in line with biblical teachings paves the way for a life dedicated to holiness. By renewing our minds, relying on the Holy Spirit, and engaging with a supportive community, we can effectively renounce sin and embrace the fullness of life that God intends for us.

In Order to Renounce Sin and Embrace Holiness

you must... "Walk Differently"

Here's an example...

A biblical character who walked differently from the world is Esther, the queen of Persia. Her story, found in the Book of Esther, showcases a woman who chose to act according to God's will, even when the world around her was driven by power, fear, and self-interest. Esther was a Jewish woman who had been chosen as queen by King Xerxes, though her identity as a Jew was unknown to him and to most of the court.

When the king's advisor, Haman, plotted to annihilate the Jewish people, Esther faced a difficult decision. She could have kept silent and protected herself, as the law forbade anyone, including the queen, from approaching the king without being summoned. However, Esther understood that her position was not just for personal gain but for such a time as this (Esther 4:14). She chose to risk her life to speak out for her people, trusting in God's sovereignty and providence.

Esther's willingness to stand apart from the world's norms of self-preservation and political maneuvering demonstrated courage and faith. She walked in obedience to God's higher calling, showing that God's ways are often counter to worldly wisdom, and His purposes often require boldness, humility, and faithfulness, even at great personal cost.

Here's some practical steps...

- Understand the teachings of the Bible as a guide for daily living.
- Embrace the principles of love, kindness, and humility.
- Prioritize spiritual growth through prayer and meditation on God's Word.
- Resist societal pressures that conflict with biblical values.
- Cultivate a community of fellow believers for support and accountability.
- Practice forgiveness and grace in interactions with others.
- Seek wisdom from biblical teachings when making decisions.
- Live out your faith through actions that reflect Christ's character.
- Share the message of hope and salvation with those around you.
- Remain steadfast in faith, even in the face of worldly challenges.

Journal Your Thoughts

IN ORDER TO RENOUNCE SIN AND EMBRACE HOLINESS

21

You Must...

"FOLLOW THE WAY OF THE EAGLE"

In Order to Renounce Sin and Embrace Holiness
you must... "Follow the Way of the Eagle"
Proverbs 30:18

According to Proverbs 30:18, embracing the path of the eagle can profoundly influence your journey towards renouncing sin and embracing holiness. The eagle, a symbol of strength, vision, and freedom, teaches us valuable lessons about rising above our challenges and temptations. By observing the eagle's behavior, we can learn to soar above the distractions and moral pitfalls that often lead us astray.

Firstly, eagles are known for their keen eyesight, allowing them to spot opportunities and threats from great distances. This ability to see clearly can be paralleled in our spiritual lives. By cultivating a discerning mindset, we can identify sinful behaviors and thoughts before they take root. This heightened awareness enables us to make conscious choices that align with our values and beliefs, steering us away from actions that compromise our integrity.

Moreover, eagles are solitary creatures that often prefer to fly alone. This aspect of their nature encourages us to seek solitude and reflection in our own lives. In moments of quiet contemplation, we can assess our actions and motivations, allowing us to confront the sins that may be holding us back. This introspection fosters a deeper connection with our spiritual selves, guiding us toward a more holy existence.

Additionally, eagles are known for their ability to rise above storms. When faced with adversity, they do not shy away but instead use the winds to elevate themselves higher. This resilience is crucial in our battle against sin. Instead of succumbing to temptation or despair, we can learn to harness our struggles as opportunities for growth. By facing our challenges head-on, we can emerge stronger and more committed to living a life of holiness.

In conclusion, following the way of the eagle inspires us to develop clarity, seek solitude, and embrace resilience. By embodying these qualities, we can effectively renounce sin and cultivate a life that reflects our highest spiritual aspirations. The eagle's journey serves as a powerful metaphor for our own, reminding us that we have the capacity to rise above and embrace a path of holiness.

IN ORDER TO RENOUNCE SIN AND EMBRACE HOLINESS
YOU MUST... "FOLLOW THE WAY OF THE EAGLE"

Here's an example...

A biblical character who followed "the way of the eagle" is Moses, a leader who soared in faith and perseverance, rising above the challenges he faced in leading the Israelites from slavery to the Promised Land. Like the eagle, Moses was called to rise to great heights of leadership, guided by God's direction and empowered by His strength.

Moses' journey was marked by moments of immense challenge—leading a rebellious and often disobedient people through the wilderness, confronting Pharaoh, and dealing with constant doubts. Yet, despite the difficulties, Moses exemplified unwavering obedience to God, trusting His guidance even when the path was unclear.

One striking moment of Moses' "soaring" faith is found in Exodus 14 when the Israelites were trapped between the Red Sea and Pharaoh's army. Rather than succumbing to fear or doubt, Moses stood firm, declaring, "The Lord will fight for you; you need only to be still."

Moses followed the way of the eagle in his strength, courage, and vision. He rose above the obstacles through faith in God's promises, leading God's people with integrity and humility.

Here's some practical steps...

- Explore the biblical principles that guide the way of an eagle.
- Examine scriptural references that highlight the characteristics of eagles.
- Discuss the significance of strength and resilience as depicted in the Bible.
- Analyze the metaphor of eagles in relation to spiritual growth and renewal.
- Identify key verses that encourage believers to emulate the eagle's flight.
- Reflect on the importance of vision and perspective in a believer's life.
- Consider the role of faith in soaring above challenges.
- Highlight the connection between eagles and divine protection in Scripture.
- Encourage others to adopt the eagle's qualities in their daily walk with God.
- Summarize the lessons learned from the eagle's way as a model to follow.

Journal Your Thoughts

In Order to Renounce Sin and Embrace Holiness

22

You Must...

"OBEY THE TRUTH"

In Order to Renounce Sin and Embrace Holiness
you must... "Obey the Truth"
Galatians 5:7-10

Recognizing the truth of God's Word, as highlighted in Galatians 5:7-10, empowers individuals to reject sin and strive for a life of holiness. When we immerse ourselves in Scripture, we gain a deeper understanding of God's character, His desires for us, and the nature of sin itself. This knowledge serves as a guiding light, illuminating the path toward righteousness and away from the darkness of wrongdoing.

The teachings found in the Bible provide not only moral guidance but also the strength to resist temptation. By internalizing these truths, we develop a spiritual foundation that helps us recognize the fleeting nature of sinful pleasures. The more we align our thoughts and actions with God's Word, the more we cultivate a desire for holiness. This shift in focus allows us to see sin for what it truly is—a barrier to our relationship with God and a hindrance to our spiritual growth.

Moreover, engaging with Scripture fosters a sense of accountability. When we understand the principles laid out in the Bible, we become more aware of our choices and their consequences. This awareness encourages us to make decisions that reflect our commitment to living a holy life. The stories of biblical figures who faced temptation and chose righteousness serve as powerful examples, inspiring us to follow in their footsteps.

Prayer and meditation on God's Word further enhance this process. As we seek His guidance, we invite the Holy Spirit to work within us, transforming our hearts and minds. This divine assistance is crucial in our battle against sin, as it equips us with the wisdom and strength needed to overcome challenges.

Ultimately, adhering to the truth of God's Word is not merely about following rules; it is about cultivating a relationship with God. This relationship empowers us to renounce sin and embrace holiness, leading to a life filled with purpose, joy, and fulfillment. By committing ourselves to the truth of Scripture, we embark on a journey that not only changes us but also reflects God's love and grace to the world around us.

IN ORDER TO RENOUNCE SIN AND EMBRACE HOLINESS
YOU MUST... "OBEY THE TRUTH"

Here's an example...

One biblical character who exemplified obedience to God's Word is Joshua, the successor of Moses and leader of Israel as they entered the Promised Land. In the book of Joshua, we see his unwavering commitment to following God's commands, even in difficult circumstances. After the death of Moses, God instructed Joshua to lead the Israelites into Canaan and promised to be with him as He had been with Moses (Joshua 1:5-9). Joshua's obedience to God's commands is evident in his actions, particularly in his role in the conquest of Jericho.

In Joshua 6, when God gave the Israelites a seemingly unconventional battle plan to march around the city of Jericho for seven days, Joshua obeyed without question. The walls of Jericho fell as a result of their faith and obedience to God's instruction, demonstrating Joshua's trust in God's Word. Throughout his leadership, Joshua emphasized the importance of obeying God's laws. In Joshua 1:7-8, he repeatedly encouraged the people to meditate on God's Word day and night, ensuring their success and prosperity.

At the end of his life, Joshua famously declared, "As for me and my house, we will serve the Lord" (Joshua 24:15), showing his lifelong commitment to following God's Word and leading others to do the same.

Here's some practical steps...

- Understand the importance of God's Word as the ultimate truth.
- Study the Scriptures regularly to gain insight and wisdom.
- Apply biblical teachings to daily life decisions and actions.
- Seek guidance through prayer for understanding and strength.
- Embrace accountability by sharing your journey with fellow believers.
- Reflect on personal beliefs and align them with biblical principles.
- Practice humility and openness to correction from God's Word.
- Live out the teachings of Jesus in interactions with others.
- Cultivate a heart of gratitude and worship in response to God's truth.
- Share the truth of God's Word with others to encourage their faith.

Journal Your Thoughts

IN ORDER TO RENOUNCE SIN AND EMBRACE HOLINESS

23

You Must...

"BE RECEPTIVE TO GUIDANCE"

In Order to Renounce Sin and Embrace Holiness

you must... "Be Receptive to Guidance"
Proverbs 19:20

Embracing guidance can profoundly transform your journey towards renouncing sin and welcoming holiness into your life. When you allow a guiding force—be it a mentor, spiritual leader, or even a set of principles—to steer your actions and decisions, you create a supportive framework that encourages positive change. This guidance acts as a beacon, illuminating the path away from temptation and towards a life of virtue.

Firstly, guidance provides clarity. In moments of confusion or moral dilemma, having someone to turn to can help you discern right from wrong. This clarity is essential in recognizing the subtle ways sin can infiltrate your life. By understanding these nuances, you become more equipped to resist them. A mentor can share their experiences and insights, helping you to see the consequences of sin and the beauty of living a holy life.

Moreover, guidance fosters accountability. When you share your goals and struggles with someone who supports your journey, you create a sense of responsibility. This accountability can motivate you to stay committed to your path, even when faced with challenges. Knowing that someone is there to encourage you and hold you accountable can make a significant difference in your resolve to renounce sin.

Additionally, guidance nurtures a sense of community. Engaging with others who share similar values and aspirations can reinforce your commitment to holiness. This community can provide encouragement, share wisdom, and celebrate your progress, making the journey feel less isolating. Together, you can uplift one another, creating an environment where holiness is not just a personal goal but a shared mission.

Finally, according to Proverbs 19:20, allowing guidance into your life opens your heart to transformation. It encourages you to reflect on your actions and intentions, fostering a deeper understanding of what it means to live a holy life. This reflection can lead to genuine repentance and a desire to grow closer to your ideals. By embracing guidance, you not only renounce sin but also cultivate a life rich in purpose and fulfillment.

In Order to Renounce Sin and Embrace Holiness

you must... "Be Receptive to Guidance"

Here's an example...

One biblical character who was open to advice is Rehoboam, the son of Solomon and the king of Israel. In 1 Kings 12, when Rehoboam ascended the throne after his father's death, he was faced with a decision on how to handle the grievances of the people who had been burdened by heavy taxes during Solomon's reign. Initially, Rehoboam sought the counsel of his father's advisers, the older men who had served Solomon. They recommended that he lighten the yoke on the people and win their loyalty. However, Rehoboam also consulted with his younger, more inexperienced friends who advised him to impose even harsher conditions to assert his authority.

Although Rehoboam initially followed the advice of his peers, leading to a rebellion and the splitting of the kingdom, his story reveals a critical lesson about the importance of seeking wise counsel. Despite his failure, the Bible highlights the significance of being open to advice from those who have experience and wisdom. Later, Rehoboam showed some humility by seeking guidance from the prophet Shemaiah in times of crisis (1 Kings 12:22-24). This openness to prophetic counsel reflects an important lesson in leadership: the value of seeking diverse, godly advice when making decisions, especially in times of uncertainty.

Here's some practical steps...

- Seek wisdom from Scripture as a foundation for receiving advice.
- Embrace humility to recognize the value of others' insights.
- Pray for discernment to understand and accept guidance.
- Listen actively to counsel without preconceived notions.
- Reflect on Proverbs, which emphasizes the importance of wise counsel.
- Surround yourself with trusted individuals who offer godly advice.
- Be willing to adjust your perspective based on biblical teachings.
- Acknowledge that guidance may come from unexpected sources.
- Practice gratitude for the advice received, viewing it as a blessing.
- Commit to applying the guidance in your life for spiritual growth.

Journal Your Thoughts

In Order to Renounce Sin and Embrace Holiness

24

You Must...

"DISREGARD THE OPINIONS OF OTHERS"

In Order to Renounce Sin and Embrace Holiness

you must... "Disregard the Opinions of Others"
Proverbs 29:25

Disregarding the opinions of others can be a powerful step toward renouncing sin and embracing a life of holiness. In a world filled with external influences and societal pressures, it's easy to get swayed by what others think or say, as highlighted in Proverbs 29:25. However, when we prioritize our own convictions and values over the judgments of those around us, we create a pathway to spiritual growth and integrity.

When we focus on our personal beliefs and the teachings that resonate with our spirit, we begin to cultivate a deeper understanding of what it means to live a holy life. This journey often requires us to step away from the noise of public opinion and instead listen to our inner voice, which is often aligned with our higher purpose. By doing so, we can identify the sins that may have been normalized by society but are contrary to our spiritual aspirations.

Moreover, disregarding the opinions of others allows us to break free from the chains of conformity. Many people find themselves engaging in sinful behaviors simply to fit in or gain approval. When we choose to stand firm in our beliefs, we not only reject these temptations but also inspire others to do the same. This act of courage can create a ripple effect, encouraging a community that values holiness over societal acceptance.

Additionally, embracing our own convictions fosters resilience. When we are grounded in our faith and values, we become less susceptible to guilt or shame that may arise from the judgments of others. This inner strength empowers us to pursue a life that reflects our true selves, leading us away from sin and toward a more fulfilling existence.

Ultimately, by disregarding the opinions of others, we open ourselves up to a world of new opportunities. This choice not only helps us renounce sin but also allows us to embrace a life of holiness, authenticity, and purpose. It is in this space of self-acceptance and spiritual clarity that we can truly thrive.

In Order to Renounce Sin and Embrace Holiness
You Must... "Disregard the Opinions of Others"

Here's an example...

A biblical character who disregarded the opinions of others and boldly followed God's calling is Rahab, a prostitute living in Jericho, whose story is found in Joshua 2. When the Israelite spies came to Jericho, Rahab hid them from the king's soldiers, despite the great personal risk to herself. Her actions were driven by her belief in the God of Israel, whom she had heard of and acknowledged as the one true God. In her conversation with the spies, Rahab boldly declared, "I know that the Lord has given you this land...for the Lord your God is God in heaven above and on the earth below" (Joshua 2:9, 11).

By sheltering the spies, Rahab defied her city, her culture, and even the moral expectations of her own profession. She put her trust in God's plan over the opinions of those around her. Her faith and courage led to her and her family's salvation when the Israelites eventually conquered Jericho.

Rahab's disregard for the opinions of others and her willingness to act according to her faith demonstrate a remarkable courage and obedience to God. Her actions are a reminder that sometimes following God's will requires stepping out of societal norms, regardless of judgment or fear of consequences. Rahab's faith ultimately made her an ancestor of Jesus (Matthew 1:5), highlighting the transformative power of obedience to God.

Here's some practical steps...

- Understand the importance of seeking God's approval over human opinions.
- Reflect on Proverbs 29:25, which warns against the fear of man.
- Emphasize the need for personal conviction rooted in Scripture.
- Recognize that Jesus faced criticism and remained focused on His mission.
- Study Gal. 1:10, which highlights the priority of pleasing God over people.
- Acknowledge that not all advice aligns with biblical truth.
- Cultivate a strong prayer life to discern God's voice amidst others' opinions.
- Surround yourself with wise counsel that aligns with biblical teachings.
- Remember that your identity is found in Christ, not in others' perceptions.
- Trust in God's plan for your life, regardless of external judgments.

Journal Your Thoughts

In Order to Renounce Sin and Embrace Holiness

25

You Must...

"BE UNCOMPROMISING"

In Order to Renounce Sin and Embrace Holiness
you must... "Be Uncompromising"
Psalm 141

To truly renounce sin and embrace holiness, one must adopt an uncompromising stance against the moral failings that permeate our world, as the Psalmist did in Psalm 141. This unwavering commitment serves as a powerful catalyst for personal transformation. When we refuse to accept the sins that surround us, we create a clear boundary between our values and the temptations that seek to lead us astray.

By recognizing the destructive nature of sin, we cultivate a deeper understanding of its consequences—not just for ourselves, but for those around us. This awareness fosters a sense of responsibility, urging us to seek a higher standard of living. When we stand firm against the allure of worldly pleasures, we begin to align our actions with our spiritual aspirations. This alignment is crucial; it allows us to shed the weight of guilt and shame that often accompanies sinful behavior.

Moreover, being uncompromising in our stance against sin empowers us to make conscious choices that reflect our commitment to holiness. Each decision becomes an opportunity to reinforce our values and strengthen our resolve. As we practice this discipline, we find that our desires shift. The things that once tempted us lose their appeal, replaced by a longing for a life that honors our spiritual beliefs.

In this journey, community plays a vital role. Surrounding ourselves with like-minded individuals who share our commitment to holiness can provide support and encouragement. Together, we can hold each other accountable, celebrating victories and navigating challenges. This collective strength amplifies our resolve, making it easier to resist the pull of sin.

Ultimately, embracing holiness is not merely about avoiding sin; it's about actively pursuing a life filled with purpose, love, and integrity. By being uncompromising in our rejection of worldly sins, we open ourselves to a transformative experience that leads us closer to our true selves. In this pursuit, we discover the profound joy and peace that come from living a life aligned with our highest values.

In Order to Renounce Sin and Embrace Holiness
you must... "Be Uncompromising"

Here's an example...

A powerful example of unwavering commitment to God is found in the life of Shadrach, Meshach, and Abednego, three Hebrew youths who were taken into Babylonian captivity. In Daniel 3, King Nebuchadnezzar ordered all people to worship a golden image he had set up, under penalty of death by being thrown into a fiery furnace. Despite the pressure to conform, Shadrach, Meshach, and Abednego refused to bow down to the idol, demonstrating their uncompromising commitment to God.

When confronted by the king, they boldly declared, "If we are thrown into the blazing furnace, the God we serve is able to deliver us from it, and he will deliver us from Your Majesty's hand. But even if he does not, we want you to know, Your Majesty, that we will not serve your gods or worship the image of gold you have set up" (Daniel 3:17-18).

Their refusal to worship anything other than the true God, even in the face of certain death, exemplifies an uncompromising devotion to God's commands. Miraculously, God preserved them from the flames, and they emerged unharmed. Their steadfast faith in the midst of intense pressure serves as a powerful example of remaining true to God, no matter the cost.

Here's some practical steps...

- Understand the importance of unwavering faith in God.
- Study biblical teachings that emphasize living a life of integrity.
- Commit to prayer and seek guidance from the Holy Spirit for daily decisions.
- Surround yourself with people who encourage steadfastness in faith.
- Practice obedience to God's commandments as a reflection of your devotion.
- Resist societal pressures that conflict with biblical values and principles.
- Engage in regular Scripture reading to strengthen your understanding.
- Demonstrate love and compassion while standing firm in your beliefs.
- Share your faith boldly, even in challenging situations, to inspire others.
- Trust in God's promises and remain steadfast in your commitment to Him.

Journal Your Thoughts

In Order to Renounce Sin and Embrace Holiness

26

You Must...

"ADHERE TO THE GOLDEN RULE"

In Order to Renounce Sin and Embrace Holiness

you must... "Adhere to the Golden Rule"
Matthew 7:12

Embracing the Bible's golden rule, as emphasized in in Matthew 7:12, which urges us to treat others as we wish to be treated, can significantly influence our journey toward rejecting sin and embracing a life of holiness. This principle acts as a beacon, guiding us toward a more virtuous existence. By making this rule a part of our lives, we foster empathy and compassion, which are vital in overcoming sinful tendencies.

When we consciously choose to show kindness and respect to those around us, we begin to shift our attention away from self-serving desires that often lead to sinful actions. Rather than engaging in behaviors that may harm ourselves or others, we start to prioritize the well-being of our community. This change in mindset nurtures a sense of connection and responsibility, making it easier to resist temptations that could lead us off course.

Furthermore, the golden rule prompts us to reflect on our actions and their effects on others. By considering how our choices impact those we encounter, we become more aware of our behavior. This awareness is essential for identifying and letting go of sinful habits. When we ask ourselves, "Would I want to be treated this way?" we are encouraged to rethink actions that may not align with a life of holiness.

Additionally, living by this principle fosters a spirit of forgiveness and understanding. We learn to offer grace to others, just as we hope to receive grace ourselves. This practice not only deepens our relationships but also helps us release grudges and resentment, which can hinder our pursuit of holiness.

In summary, following the golden rule steers us away from wrongdoing and leads us toward a life enriched with virtue. It inspires us to embody love, compassion, and integrity in our everyday interactions. As we strive to treat others with the kindness and respect we seek for ourselves, we find ourselves drawing closer to the ideals of holiness, ultimately reflecting God's love in our lives.

In Order to Renounce Sin and Embrace Holiness
you must... "Adhere to the Golden Rule"

Here's an example...

The Parable of the Good Samaritan, found in Luke 10:25-37, is a powerful illustration of the Golden Rule: "Do to others as you would have them do to you" (Luke 6:31). In the story, Jesus describes a man who was traveling from Jerusalem to Jericho and was attacked by robbers. Left half-dead by the side of the road, the man was ignored by a priest and a Levite—religious figures who, despite their positions, failed to show compassion or aid.

However, a Samaritan, someone considered an enemy by the Jewish people of the time, stopped to help. He bandaged the man's wounds, placed him on his donkey, took him to an inn, and paid for his care. The Samaritan's actions exemplified the Golden Rule by treating the wounded man with the kindness, compassion, and care that he himself would hope for in a time of need.

The Samaritan did not let societal divisions or personal inconvenience prevent him from doing what was right. His response was driven by love and empathy, not by expectations of reward or recognition. Jesus used this parable to teach that loving our neighbor transcends cultural and religious boundaries, and true adherence to the Golden Rule is shown through practical, selfless acts of kindness toward others, regardless of their background or status.

Here's some practical steps...

- Understand the essence of the Golden Rule.
- Reflect on biblical teachings that emphasize love and mercy towards others.
- Explore Matthew 7:12, which directly states the Golden Rule.
- Study Jesus' teachings and how they apply to daily interactions.
- Practice empathy by putting yourself in others' shoes.
- Keep an eye on your actions to make sure they follow the Golden Rule.
- Encourage community and relationships built on mutual respect.
- Share the principle with others to promote a culture of understanding.
- Apply the Golden Rule in challenging situations to foster resolution.
- Commit to living out this principle consistently in all areas of life.

Journal Your Thoughts

In Order to Renounce Sin and Embrace Holiness

27

You Must...

"DESIRE GOD'S PRESENCE"

In Order to Renounce Sin and Embrace Holiness

you must... "Desire God's Presence"
Psalm 15

Experiencing the presence of God can profoundly transform our lives, guiding us away from sin and toward a life of holiness. When we actively seek to dwell in God's presence, as the Psalmist did in Psalm 15, we open ourselves to His love, grace, and guidance, which empowers us to make choices that align with His will.

First and foremost, being in God's presence fosters a deep sense of awareness of His holiness. This awareness can illuminate the areas of our lives that fall short of His standards, as highlighted in Isaiah 6:5. As we draw closer to God, we begin to see our sins not just as mistakes, but as barriers that hinder our relationship with Him. This realization can ignite a desire within us to renounce those sins, as we long for a more intimate connection with the Lord.

Moreover, God's presence brings about a transformative power that can reshape our desires. When we immerse ourselves in prayer, worship, and the study of His Word, we cultivate a heart that yearns for righteousness. The more we experience God's love and mercy, the more we are compelled to reflect those qualities in our own lives. This shift in focus helps us to embrace holiness, as we begin to prioritize our relationship with God over fleeting pleasures that lead us astray.

Additionally, being in God's presence provides us with the strength to resist temptation. In moments of weakness, we can call upon the Holy Spirit, who empowers us to overcome sinful inclinations. The support of a vibrant spiritual life, filled with community and accountability, further reinforces our commitment to holiness. Surrounding ourselves with fellow believers who encourage us in our faith can help us stay focused on our spiritual journey.

Ultimately, experiencing God's presence is a profound and life-changing event that leads us to renounce sin and embrace a life of holiness. It is through this divine connection that we find the strength, motivation, and clarity needed to pursue a life that reflects God's love and righteousness.

In Order to Renounce Sin and Embrace Holiness
you must... "Desire God's Presence"

Here's an example...

One biblical character who profoundly desired God's presence is Hannah, the mother of Samuel. Found in 1 Samuel 1, Hannah's story demonstrates an earnest longing for divine closeness and intervention. Barren and deeply distressed by her inability to conceive, Hannah fervently prayed at the temple, vowing that if God granted her a son, she would dedicate him to the Lord's service for life (1 Samuel 1:11). Her prayer was not only for a child but for God's presence and favor to be upon her life in a deeply personal way.

Hannah's desire was not for selfish reasons; she sought God's presence to fulfill her spiritual longing and to honor Him. When God answered her prayer and she bore Samuel, she rejoiced with a beautiful song of thanksgiving in 1 Samuel 2, acknowledging God's sovereignty and faithfulness. Hannah's longing was not just for a miracle but for a restored relationship with God and the fulfillment of her vow. She exemplifies a deep yearning for God's presence in times of personal suffering and struggle, and her story highlights how God's presence can bring transformation and hope. Hannah's commitment to dedicating her son to God shows her deep trust and recognition of God's sovereignty in her life.

Here's some practical steps...

- Explore the significance of seeking God's presence as outlined in Scripture.
- Understand the importance of prayer as a means to connect with God.
- Reflect on the role of worship in drawing closer to God's presence.
- Study biblical passages that emphasize the desire for God's nearness.
- Consider the impact of meditation on God's Word in fostering His presence.
- Acknowledge the importance of community and fellowship in seeking God.
- Embrace a lifestyle of obedience to align with God's will.
- Cultivate a heart of gratitude to recognize God's presence in daily life.
- Engage in fasting as a spiritual discipline to deepen your desire for God.
- Seek guidance from the Holy Spirit to enhance your pursuit of God.

Journal Your Thoughts

In Order to Renounce Sin and Embrace Holiness

28

You Must...

"GET BACK TO THE BASICS"

In Order to Renounce Sin and Embrace Holiness

you must... "Get Back to the Basics"

Romans 12:2

Returning to the fundamentals of faith in God can profoundly transform our lives, guiding us away from sin and toward a path of holiness. Romans 12:2 emphasizes the importance of transforming one's mindset to align with God's will rather than conforming to worldly values. In a world filled with distractions and temptations, it's easy to lose sight of our spiritual foundation. However, by reconnecting with the core principles of our faith, we can find the strength to renounce sinful behaviors and cultivate a life that reflects divine values.

At the heart of faith lies a relationship with God, built on trust, love, and obedience. When we prioritize this relationship, we begin to see the world through a different lens. The teachings of Scripture remind us of the importance of living a life that honors God. By immersing ourselves in prayer, worship, and the study of Scriptures, we reinforce our commitment to righteousness. This spiritual nourishment empowers us to resist the allure of sin, as we become more attuned to the voice of God guiding us toward holiness.

Moreover, embracing the basics of faith fosters a sense of community and accountability. Surrounding ourselves with fellow believers encourages us to share our struggles and victories. In this supportive environment, we can openly discuss our challenges with sin and seek guidance from those who share our values. This collective journey strengthens our resolve and inspires us to pursue a life that reflects God's love and grace.

Additionally, returning to the basics helps us cultivate a heart of gratitude and humility. Recognizing the sacrifices made for our salvation reminds us of the importance of living a life that honors that gift. As we grow in our understanding of God's mercy, we become more motivated to turn away from sin and embrace a lifestyle that seeks to glorify Him.

In conclusion, getting back to the basics of faith in God is a powerful catalyst for renouncing sin and embracing holiness. By nurturing our relationship with God, engaging with our community, and fostering a spirit of gratitude, we can transform our lives and reflect the light of Christ in a world that desperately needs it.

In Order to Renounce Sin and Embrace Holiness
you must... "Get Back to the Basics"

Here's an example...

A biblical character who returned to the fundamental tenets of faith is Hezekiah, the king of Judah. His story is primarily found in 2 Kings 18-20 and 2 Chronicles 29-32. Hezekiah ascended to the throne at a time when Judah had strayed far from God, with idolatry and corruption rampant in the nation. Hezekiah's reign marked a radical return to the core principles of worship and trust in God.

Upon becoming king, Hezekiah immediately removed the high places, shattered sacred pillars, and cut down the Asherah poles—idolatrous practices that had crept into Judah. He reopened the doors of the temple, which had been closed due to neglect, and restored the Levitical priesthood, calling the people back to true worship. In 2 Chronicles 29, he reinstituted the Passover, which had not been celebrated properly for years, and encouraged the people to renew their covenant with God.

Hezekiah's faith was tested when the Assyrian king, Sennacherib, threatened to destroy Judah. Rather than relying on military might, Hezekiah turned to God in prayer, reminding God of His promises to protect His people (2 Kings 19:14-19). His return to the basics of trusting in God's power and seeking His guidance resulted in divine deliverance.

Here's some practical steps...

- Explore the core principles of faith as outlined in the Holy Bible.
- Identify passages that emphasize the importance of foundational beliefs.
- Reflect on the teachings of Jesus and their relevance to your life.
- Discuss the significance of prayer and Scripture study in strengthening faith.
- Encourage participation in community worship to reinforce shared beliefs.
- Highlight the role of repentance and forgiveness in returning to faith.
- Examine the importance of love and mercy as central tenets of Christianity.
- Promote the practice of living out faith through actions and service to others.
- Suggest resources for deeper understanding of biblical teachings.
- Urge individuals to seek guidance from spiritual leaders and mentors.

Journal Your Thoughts

In Order to Renounce Sin and Embrace Holiness

29

You Must...

"PRAISE GOD"

In Order to Renounce Sin and Embrace Holiness

you must... "Praise God"

Psalm 138

Praising God, as highlighted in Psalm 138, serves as a powerful catalyst for renouncing sin and embracing a life of holiness. When we lift our voices in worship and gratitude, we shift our focus from the temptations and distractions of the world to the divine nature of God. This act of praise not only acknowledges His greatness but also reminds us of His unwavering love and mercy.

Engaging in heartfelt worship fosters a deeper connection with God, allowing us to experience His presence in profound ways. As we meditate on His attributes—His faithfulness, goodness, and righteousness—we begin to see our own shortcomings in a new light. This awareness can lead to genuine repentance, as we recognize the areas in our lives that do not align with His holiness. The more we praise Him, the more we desire to reflect His character in our own lives.

Moreover, praising God cultivates a spirit of gratitude, which can transform our perspective. When we focus on the blessings and grace we have received, we become less inclined to indulge in sinful behaviors that may have once tempted us. Gratitude shifts our priorities, encouraging us to seek fulfillment in our relationship with God rather than in fleeting pleasures that lead to spiritual emptiness.

Additionally, worshiping God strengthens our resolve to pursue holiness. As we declare His greatness, we are reminded of the power He has to help us overcome sin. This acknowledgment builds our faith, empowering us to resist temptation and make choices that honor Him. The more we immerse ourselves in praise, the more we are equipped to live out our calling as His children, reflecting His light in a world that often embraces darkness.

In essence, praising God is not just an act of worship; it is a transformative practice that leads us away from sin and toward a life characterized by holiness. By continually lifting our hearts in praise, we align ourselves with His will and become vessels of His love and grace.

In Order to Renounce Sin and Embrace Holiness

you must... "Praise God"

Here's an example...

A biblical character who worshiped and praised God is Job. Job's story, found in the book that bears his name, is one of profound faith, suffering, and unwavering devotion to God. Job was a man who experienced incredible loss—his wealth, his health, and his children all perished in a series of devastating events. Yet, despite his immense suffering, Job's response was an outpouring of praise and worship to God.

In Job 1:20-21, after hearing of the tragic deaths of his children and the loss of his possessions, Job tore his clothes, shaved his head, and fell to the ground in worship. He said, "Naked I came from my mother's womb, and naked I will depart. The Lord gave and the Lord has taken away; may the name of the Lord be praised." Job's acknowledgment of God's sovereignty, even in the face of personal calamity, demonstrates his deep reverence and trust.

Later, after enduring even greater physical affliction and hearing the challenging words of his friends, Job continued to seek God, expressing both his sorrow and his longing for divine understanding. Ultimately, Job's worship was not rooted in circumstances, but in his acknowledgment of God's authority, goodness, and power—revealing a faith that praised God in both joy and suffering.

Here's some practical steps...

- Understand the importance of praise in the Bible as a form of worship.
- Read Psalms to find examples of how to express gratitude and adoration.
- Use music and singing as a means to glorify God.
- Engage in prayer, incorporating praise and thanksgiving.
- Acknowledge God's attributes in your praises and prayers.
- Share testimonies of God's goodness in your life to inspire others.
- Participate in communal worship, joining with others to lift praises together.
- Reflect on God's creation and His works as a basis for your praise.
- Practice humility and reverence when approaching God in praise.
- Make praise a daily habit, integrating it into your routine and lifestyle.

Journal Your Thoughts

In Order to Renounce Sin and Embrace Holiness

30

You Must...

"REHEARSE GOD'S HOLINESS"

In Order to Renounce Sin and Embrace Holiness

you must... "Rehearse God's Holiness"
Psalm 5:4-6

Rehearsing and repeating God's Word, particularly as highlighted in Psalm 5:4-6, serves as a powerful tool in our spiritual journey, guiding us to renounce sin and embrace holiness. This passage emphasizes the nature of God, who does not delight in wickedness and cannot tolerate evil. By immersing ourselves in these truths, we begin to align our thoughts and actions with His divine will.

When we consistently meditate on Scripture, we create a mental and spiritual framework that helps us recognize sin for what it is—an affront to God's holiness. The more we internalize His Word, the clearer our understanding becomes of what it means to live a life that pleases Him. This process of repetition acts like a spiritual filter, allowing us to discern right from wrong more effectively. As we recite and reflect on these verses, we cultivate a deeper awareness of God's character and His expectations for us.

Moreover, rehearsing God's Word strengthens our resolve against temptation. When faced with choices that could lead us astray, recalling the truths found in Scripture can provide the necessary strength to resist. It's as if we arm ourselves with divine wisdom, enabling us to stand firm against the allure of sin. This practice not only fortifies our faith but also fosters a desire for holiness, as we become increasingly aware of the beauty and joy that comes from living in accordance with God's will.

Additionally, engaging with Scripture in this way fosters a sense of accountability. We are reminded that our actions have consequences and that God's love calls us to a higher standard. As we embrace His Word, we find ourselves drawn to a life that reflects His holiness, leading us to renounce behaviors that do not align with His teachings.

Ultimately, the act of repeating and rehearsing God's Word transforms our hearts and minds, guiding us toward a life marked by righteousness and a deeper relationship with our Creator.

IN ORDER TO RENOUNCE SIN AND EMBRACE HOLINESS
YOU MUST... "REHEARSE GOD'S HOLINESS"

Here's an example...

The psalmist in Psalm 1 offers a powerful example of someone who deeply values and consistently engages with God's Word. Psalm 1 contrasts the life of the righteous with that of the wicked, highlighting the blessing that comes to those who make God's Word central to their lives. The psalmist begins by describing the righteous person as one who "delights in the law of the Lord" and meditates on it "day and night" (Psalm 1:2). This is a clear indication that the psalmist sees the act of meditating on Scripture as a continual practice—something that is not just a one-time event but a recurring and deliberate engagement with God's truth.

By describing the righteous person as like a tree "planted by streams of water", the psalmist emphasizes the stability, nourishment, and fruitfulness that come from a life rooted in God's Word. The righteous individual not only reads and quotes Scripture but rehearses it, allowing it to shape their actions, thoughts, and decisions. The psalmist's life illustrates how constant reflection on and obedience to God's Word leads to spiritual flourishing and alignment with God's holiness. This model of deep, intentional engagement with Scripture is a powerful example of how meditating on God's Word leads to lasting wisdom, peace, and fruitfulness in the life of the believer.

Here's some practical steps...

- Explore the practice of biblical meditation by focusing on Scripture passages.
- Set aside dedicated time for quiet reflection on God's Word.
- Choose specific verses that resonate with your spiritual journey.
- Examine the Scriptures you choose carefully and with intention.
- Consider the meaning and context of the verses you meditate on.
- Repeat the verses aloud or in your mind to internalize them.
- Pray for understanding and insight as you meditate on the text.
- Journal your thoughts and revelations that arise during meditation.
- Apply the teachings of the Bible to your daily life.
- Share your insights with others to encourage collective growth in faith.

Journal Your Thoughts

IN ORDER TO RENOUNCE SIN AND EMBRACE HOLINESS

31

You Must...

"DEAL WITH SIN BIBLICALLY"

In Order to Renounce Sin and Embrace Holiness

you must... "Deal With Sin Biblically"

2 Corinthians 7:1

To biblically address sin, one can turn to the teachings found in the Holy Bible, particularly in 2 Corinthians 7:1, which emphasizes the importance of purifying ourselves from all that contaminates body and spirit. This Scripture serves as a powerful reminder that the journey toward holiness begins with a conscious decision to renounce sin.

First and foremost, acknowledging sin is crucial. It requires a humble heart that recognizes the areas in life where one may have strayed from God's path. This acknowledgment is not merely about feeling guilty; it's about understanding the weight of sin and its consequences. By reflecting on our actions and their alignment with biblical teachings, we can identify what needs to change.

Next, repentance plays a vital role in this process. True repentance involves more than just saying sorry; it requires a heartfelt desire to turn away from sin and seek God's forgiveness. This act of turning away signifies a commitment to change and a willingness to embrace a life that honors God. Engaging in prayer and seeking the Holy Spirit's guidance can empower individuals to make these necessary changes.

Moreover, surrounding oneself with a supportive community is essential. Fellowship with other believers provides encouragement and accountability. Sharing struggles and victories with others can strengthen one's resolve to live a holy life. The Bible encourages believers to bear one another's burdens, fostering an environment where growth and healing can occur.

Finally, immersing oneself in Scripture is a powerful tool for combating sin. The Word of God serves as a guide, illuminating the path toward righteousness. Regularly reading and meditating on biblical passages can instill a deeper understanding of God's will and inspire a desire to live in accordance with it.

In summary, dealing with sin biblically involves acknowledgment, repentance, community support, and immersion in Scripture. By following these steps, individuals can effectively renounce sin and embrace a life of holiness, aligning themselves more closely with God's purpose.

In Order to Renounce Sin and Embrace Holiness
you must... "Deal With Sin Biblically"

Here's an example...

A biblical character who dealt with sin properly is the Apostle Peter. Peter's story illustrates the journey from sin to repentance and restoration. During the time of Jesus' arrest and trial, Peter, despite his earlier bold promises of loyalty, denied Jesus three times (Luke 22:61). This act of betrayal was a grievous sin, not just against Jesus but also against his own commitment to follow Him.

When Peter realized what he had done, he was immediately convicted. The Gospel of Luke records that "the Lord turned and looked at Peter" after the rooster crowed, and Peter wept bitterly (Luke 22:61-62). Peter's response was not one of defensiveness or blame but deep sorrow and repentance. He acknowledged his failure and recognized the weight of his sin.

After Jesus' resurrection, in a powerful moment of grace, Jesus restored Peter by asking him three times, "Do you love me?" (John 21:15-17). Each time, Peter affirmed his love, and Jesus commissioned him to feed His sheep, symbolizing Peter's full restoration and his call to lead others.

Peter's response to his sin—acknowledging it, repenting, and accepting God's grace—demonstrates a model for dealing with sin, showing that repentance leads to forgiveness and renewed purpose in God's service.

Here's some practical steps...

- Understand the nature of sin as described in the Bible.
- Acknowledge personal sin and its impact on your relationship with God.
- Repent sincerely, turning away from sin and seeking forgiveness.
- Confess sins to God, as outlined in 1 John 1:9.
- Seek accountability from fellow believers to help resist temptation.
- Study Scripture to gain insight into God's standards for living.
- Pray regularly for strength and guidance in overcoming sin.
- Embrace grace and understand that forgiveness is available through Christ.
- Cultivate a lifestyle of worship and service to reinforce spiritual growth.
- Trust in the Holy Spirit to empower you to live righteously.

Journal Your Thoughts

In Order to Renounce Sin and Embrace Holiness

32

You Must...

"ADD THE RIGHT THINGS TO YOUR LIFE"

In Order to Renounce Sin and Embrace Holiness
you must... "Add the Right Things to Your Life"
2 Peter 1:5-8

In 2 Peter 1:5-8, we are encouraged to actively incorporate specific virtues into our lives, which can profoundly impact our journey toward holiness and away from sin. This passage outlines a progression of qualities—faith, goodness, knowledge, self-control, perseverance, godliness, mutual affection, and love—that, when cultivated, can transform our character and actions.

By adding these virtues, we create a strong foundation for our spiritual growth. Faith serves as the cornerstone, allowing us to trust in God's promises and guidance. From this faith, we develop goodness, which inspires us to act with integrity and kindness. As we deepen our knowledge of God and His Word, we gain wisdom that helps us discern right from wrong, making it easier to reject sinful behaviors.

Self-control is another critical virtue that empowers us to resist temptation. In a world filled with distractions and moral challenges, practicing self-control enables us to make choices that align with our values and beliefs. This perseverance in the face of trials strengthens our resolve, helping us to remain steadfast in our commitment to holiness.

Godliness, the next quality, reflects our desire to live in a way that honors God. It encourages us to seek a lifestyle that mirrors Christ's character, further distancing us from sin. As we cultivate mutual affection and love, we foster a supportive community that encourages one another in our spiritual journeys. This sense of belonging can be a powerful motivator to renounce sin, as we desire to uplift and inspire those around us.

Ultimately, the culmination of these virtues leads to a fruitful life, as stated in the passage. When we embody these qualities, we not only grow closer to God but also become beacons of light in a world that often embraces darkness. By intentionally adding these elements to our lives, we can effectively renounce sin and embrace a life of holiness, reflecting the love and grace of our Creator.

IN ORDER TO RENOUNCE SIN AND EMBRACE HOLINESS
YOU MUST... "ADD THE RIGHT THINGS TO YOUR LIFE"

Here's an example...

One biblical character who exemplified a strong foundation of love, faith, and gentleness is Mary, the mother of Jesus. Mary's life was marked by deep faith in God and a gentle submission to His will, even when faced with uncertainty and hardship. When the angel Gabriel appeared to her and announced that she would conceive the Messiah, Mary's response was one of humility and trust: "I am the Lord's servant. May your word to me be fulfilled" (Luke 1:38). Her acceptance of God's plan demonstrated her unwavering faith, even in the midst of societal scandal and personal sacrifice.

Mary's love for Jesus was evident throughout His life. She cared for Him with tenderness as an infant, witnessed His growth, and followed Him during His ministry. At the cross, despite the agony of watching her son suffer, Mary remained present, showing the depth of her maternal love and commitment. Her gentleness was reflected not just in her role as a mother, but in her willingness to listen and ponder the things of God (Luke 2:19).

Throughout her life, Mary exemplified a foundation of love, faith, and gentleness, trusting in God's plan and demonstrating humility and devotion, making her a powerful example for believers.

Here's some practical steps...

- Explore the teachings of the Bible to understand spiritual growth.
- Engage in regular prayer to deepen your relationship with God.
- Study Scripture daily to gain wisdom and insight.
- Participate in a faith community for support and encouragement.
- Practice forgiveness to cultivate a loving heart.
- Serve others to live out your faith in action.
- Reflect on personal experiences to identify areas for growth.
- Seek guidance from spiritual leaders or mentors.
- Embrace trials as opportunities for spiritual development.
- Trust in God's plan and remain steadfast in your faith journey.

Journal Your Thoughts

In Order to Renounce Sin and Embrace Holiness

33

You Must...

"FIGHT THE GOOD FIGHT OF FAITH"

In Order to Renounce Sin and Embrace Holiness

you must... "Fight the Good Fight of Faith"
1 Timothy 6:12

Fighting the good fight of faith, as highlighted in 1 Timothy 6:12, acts as a significant driving force for renouncing sin and embracing a life of holiness. This Scripture encourages believers to actively engage in their spiritual journey, reminding them that faith is not a passive endeavor but a dynamic struggle against the temptations and distractions of the world.

When we commit to this fight, we cultivate a deeper understanding of our values and beliefs. This clarity empowers us to identify and reject sinful behaviors that may have previously gone unchecked. By focusing on our faith, we develop a stronger moral compass, guiding us away from actions that contradict our commitment to holiness. The more we immerse ourselves in the teachings of Christ and the principles of our faith, the more we are equipped to resist the allure of sin.

Moreover, engaging in this spiritual battle fosters resilience. Just as athletes train rigorously to achieve their goals, believers must also train their minds and hearts to withstand the challenges that come their way. This training involves prayer, studying Scripture, and surrounding ourselves with a supportive community. Each of these practices strengthens our resolve and fortifies our spirit, making it easier to turn away from sin and pursue a life that reflects God's holiness.

Additionally, fighting the good fight of faith instills a sense of purpose. When we recognize that our struggles are not in vain but contribute to a greater mission, we find motivation to persevere. This purpose drives us to seek holiness not just for ourselves but as a testament to our faith, inspiring others to do the same.

In conclusion, the journey of fighting the good fight of faith is integral to renouncing sin and embracing holiness. It transforms our hearts, sharpens our focus, and ignites a passion for living a life that honors God. Through this commitment, we not only grow closer to Him but also become beacons of light in a world that desperately needs it.

In Order to Renounce Sin and Embrace Holiness

you must... "Fight the Good Fight of Faith"

Here's an example...

One biblical character who fought the good fight of faith is Nehemiah. Nehemiah, a cupbearer to the Persian king Artaxerxes, exemplified unwavering determination and faith in God's calling, even in the face of great opposition. When he learned that the walls of Jerusalem were in ruins, Nehemiah was deeply moved and prayed for God's favor, asking for permission to return to Jerusalem to rebuild the city (Nehemiah 1:4–11). His faith was evident in his immediate action, seeking not only to restore the physical walls of the city but also to revive the spiritual heart of God's people.

Nehemiah faced significant opposition from enemies such as Sanballat, Tobiah, and Geshem, who mocked and plotted against him. Despite threats of violence, Nehemiah remained resolute, demonstrating both physical and spiritual endurance. He organized the people to rebuild the walls despite the odds, encouraging them to work with faith, confidence, and a sense of purpose.

Nehemiah's leadership was marked by prayer, persistence, and trust in God's provision. He kept his focus on the mission, refusing to be distracted by schemes or fears. His example of fighting the good fight of faith—steadfast in purpose, reliant on God, and unshaken by adversity—remains an inspiring model for believers today.

Here's some practical steps...

- Understand the concept of faith as outlined in the Scriptures.
- Examine biblical verses that highlight perseverance and resilience.
- Engage in regular prayer to strengthen your spiritual resolve.
- Surround yourself with a community of believers for support.
- Equip yourself with knowledge of the Word to counter challenges.
- Practice humility and seek guidance from the Holy Spirit.
- Remain steadfast in your beliefs despite trials and temptations.
- Share your faith journey to inspire others and reinforce yourself.
- Reflect on the teachings of Jesus as a model for living out your faith.
- Trust in God's promises and maintain hope in His plan for your life.

Journal Your Thoughts

In Order to Renounce Sin and Embrace Holiness

34

You Must...

"BEWARE OF MISPLACED JOY"

In Order to Renounce Sin and Embrace Holiness

you must... "Beware of Misplaced Joy"

Luke 10:17-20

In Luke 10:17-20, we see the disciples returning with joy after their mission, celebrating the power they wielded over evil spirits. However, Jesus redirects their focus, reminding them that their true source of joy should not be in their accomplishments but in their relationship with God. This passage serves as a profound lesson on the importance of being mindful of misplaced joy, which can often lead us away from holiness and into the snares of sin.

When we find joy in our achievements, status, or even spiritual victories, we risk becoming prideful and self-reliant. This misplaced joy can cloud our judgment, making it easier to overlook our shortcomings and the need for repentance. By reflecting on Jesus' words, we can learn to shift our joy from temporary successes to the eternal joy found in our identity as children of God. This shift is crucial for renouncing sin, as it fosters humility and a deeper understanding of our dependence on divine grace.

Embracing holiness requires a conscious effort to align our desires with God's will. When we recognize that true joy comes from knowing Him and being part of His kingdom, we are more likely to reject the temptations that lead us astray. This awareness helps us cultivate a heart that seeks righteousness rather than personal glory.

Moreover, being mindful of misplaced joy encourages us to engage in self-examination. It prompts us to ask ourselves where we find our happiness and whether it aligns with God's purpose for our lives. By doing so, we can identify areas where we may be compromising our values and make the necessary adjustments to live a life that reflects holiness.

In summary, by focusing on the joy that comes from our relationship with God, as highlighted in Luke 10:17-20, we can effectively renounce sin and embrace a life of holiness, leading to a more fulfilling and purpose-driven existence.

In Order to Renounce Sin and Embrace Holiness
you must... "Beware of Misplaced Joy"

Here's an example...

One biblical character who experienced misplaced joy is King Ahab of Israel. Ahab, the seventh king of Israel, is known for his reign marked by idolatry and wickedness, largely influenced by his marriage to Jezebel, a Phoenician princess who led Israel into the worship of Baal. While Ahab was a powerful ruler with material wealth and political influence, his misplaced joy stemmed from worldly pursuits and a love for things that were contrary to God's will.

A significant example of Ahab's misplaced joy occurs in the story of Naboth's vineyard (1 Kings 21). Ahab, desiring Naboth's vineyard to expand his palace garden, was initially upset when Naboth refused to sell it to him because it was his ancestral inheritance. Jezebel, Ahab's wife, orchestrated Naboth's murder, allowing Ahab to seize the land. When he took possession of the vineyard, he was filled with joy—but it was a hollow joy, rooted in sin and injustice.

God sent the prophet Elijah to confront Ahab, pronouncing judgment on him and his house. Ahab's joy was fleeting, based on earthly gain and moral compromise, rather than on righteousness or true fulfillment. His story is a tragic reminder that misplaced joy, grounded in selfish desires and sin, ultimately leads to destruction rather than lasting peace and contentment.

Here's some practical steps...

- Understand the sources of true joy as outlined in Scripture.
- Recognize that joy should stem from a relationship with God.
- Reflect on Philippians 4:4, which encourages rejoicing in the Lord always.
- Identify and avoid distractions that lead to temporary happiness.
- Embrace gratitude as a practice to cultivate genuine joy in daily life.
- Study the teachings of Jesus on joy, particularly in serving others.
- Seek wisdom to discern between fleeting pleasures and enduring joy.
- Engage in prayer and meditation to align your heart with God's purposes.
- Surround yourself with a community that fosters spiritual growth and joy.
- Remember that true joy often comes through trials (James 1:2-3).

Journal Your Thoughts

IN ORDER TO RENOUNCE SIN AND EMBRACE HOLINESS

35

You Must...

"SEEK RESTORATION"

In Order to Renounce Sin and Embrace Holiness

you must... "Seek Restoration"

Mark 6:53-56

Seeking restoration, as illustrated in Mark 6:53-56, serves as a powerful catalyst for renouncing sin and embracing holiness. In this passage, we see Jesus healing the sick and restoring hope to those in need. This act of restoration is not just physical; it symbolizes a deeper spiritual renewal that can transform our lives.

When we actively seek restoration, we open ourselves to the possibility of change. Acknowledging our brokenness and the areas where we fall short allows us to confront our sins honestly. This confrontation is the first step toward repentance, which is essential for spiritual growth. Just as the people in the passage sought out Jesus for healing, we too must seek Him to heal our spiritual wounds. This pursuit of restoration encourages us to let go of our sinful habits and behaviors that distance us from God.

Moreover, embracing holiness becomes more attainable when we focus on restoration. Holiness is not merely about adhering to a set of rules; it is about cultivating a relationship with God that transforms our hearts and minds. As we seek restoration, we invite the Holy Spirit to work within us, guiding us toward a life that reflects God's love and righteousness. This divine influence empowers us to make choices that align with our faith, steering us away from sin and toward a life of holiness.

Additionally, the communal aspect of seeking restoration cannot be overlooked. In Mark 6:53-56, we see crowds coming together to seek Jesus. This reminds us of the importance of community in our spiritual journeys. Surrounding ourselves with fellow believers who encourage and support our pursuit of holiness can strengthen our resolve to renounce sin. Together, we can share our struggles and victories, fostering an environment where restoration thrives.

In conclusion, seeking restoration as illustrated in Mark 6:53-56 is a profound experience that enables us to renounce sin and embrace holiness. By acknowledging our need for healing, inviting the Holy Spirit into our lives, and engaging with a supportive community, we can experience profound spiritual renewal.

In Order to Renounce Sin and Embrace Holiness
you must... "Seek Restoration"

Here's an example...

One biblical character who sought restoration from God is King Manasseh of Judah. Manasseh initially followed a path of great wickedness, doing "evil in the eyes of the Lord" (2 Kings 21:2). He led Judah into idolatry, rebuilding the high places, erecting altars to Baal, and even sacrificing his own son to pagan gods (2 Kings 21:6). His reign brought immense corruption and sin to the nation, and it was said that he "seduced [Judah] to do more evil than the nations the Lord had destroyed before the Israelites" (2 Kings 21:9).

However, after being captured by the Assyrians and taken into captivity, Manasseh experienced a dramatic turn in his heart. In his distress, he "humbled himself greatly before the God of his ancestors" and prayed for God's mercy (2 Chronicles 33:12). God, in His infinite grace, heard Manasseh's prayer and allowed him to return to Jerusalem, where he sought to undo the damage he had caused. He removed foreign idols, repaired the altar of the Lord, and encouraged Judah to serve the true God (2 Chronicles 33:14-16).

Manasseh's story is a powerful testament to God's restorative grace, showing that even those who have wandered far from God can experience redemption when they truly repent and seek restoration through His mercy.

Here's some practical steps...

- Explore the concept of restoration as presented in the Holy Bible.
- Identify key biblical passages that discuss the theme of restoration.
- Understand the importance of repentance in the restoration process.
- Examine the role of faith and trust in God for personal renewal.
- Discuss the significance of prayer in seeking restoration.
- Highlight the impact of community and fellowship in the restoration journey.
- Reflect on the transformative power of God's grace in healing.
- Consider the importance of forgiveness, both giving and receiving.
- Analyze the steps to take for spiritual and emotional restoration.
- Encourage a commitment to living a restored life in alignment with God.

Journal Your Thoughts

In Order to Renounce Sin and Embrace Holiness

36

You Must...

"SPEAK UP BOLDLY"

In Order to Renounce Sin and Embrace Holiness
you must... "Speak Up Boldly"
2 Corinthians 4:13

Expressing your beliefs with confidence can be a life-changing experience, particularly when rooted in the wisdom of 2 Corinthians 4:13. This Scripture highlights the significance of faith and the strength found in vocalizing your convictions. By sharing your beliefs, you not only validate your own understanding but also inspire those around you. This courageous expression serves as a powerful reminder of your dedication to living a life of holiness.

When you articulate your beliefs, it deepens your comprehension of morality. This newfound clarity allows you to pinpoint areas in your life where negative influences may be present. By vocalizing your values, you establish a mental and spiritual framework that motivates you to reject sinful actions. With a clear set of principles guiding your behavior, recognizing temptations and distractions becomes much easier.

Moreover, voicing your beliefs fosters a sense of accountability. When you articulate your values to others, you invite them to accompany you on your spiritual journey. This network of support can be vital as you strive to maintain your dedication to holiness. Friends and fellow believers can offer motivation, challenge your perspectives, and help you stay focused, minimizing the chances of straying from your intended path. By sharing your faith, you also strengthen your resolve, becoming more conscious of how your actions and words impact those around you.

Additionally, confidently sharing your convictions can spark personal growth. It encourages you to explore your faith more deeply, leading to a richer comprehension of its principles. This exploration often reveals the profound beauty of holiness and the joy that comes from living a life aligned with higher values. As your insights expand, you become more adept at resisting temptation and making choices that reflect your commitment to a sacred way of life.

Ultimately, speaking boldly about your beliefs is not merely an act of bravery; it is an essential step toward rejecting sin and embracing a life of holiness.

IN ORDER TO RENOUNCE SIN AND EMBRACE HOLINESS
YOU MUST... "SPEAK UP BOLDLY"

Here's an example...

One biblical character who boldly proclaimed the Word of God is Amos, a prophet from the 8th century BCE. Amos was a shepherd and a fig tree farmer from the southern kingdom of Judah, but he was called by God to deliver a powerful message to the northern kingdom of Israel. Despite his humble background, Amos fearlessly declared God's judgment on Israel's social injustice, corruption, and idolatry. He was not a professional prophet but spoke with authority, declaring that God would punish Israel for their hypocrisy, exploiting the poor, and neglecting true worship.

Amos is best known for his blunt and direct style, using vivid imagery and parables to convey God's wrath. In Amos 5:24, he famously proclaimed, "But let justice roll on like a river, righteousness like a never-failing stream!" This call for justice highlighted the nation's moral decay and their need for repentance.

Despite opposition, Amos remained unwavering in his mission, even when faced with threats from religious authorities who sought to silence him. His courage and boldness in proclaiming God's truth serve as a powerful example of standing firm in faith, regardless of societal pressures or personal consequences.

Here's some practical steps...

- Understand the importance of speaking up for truth.
- Study biblical examples of individuals who spoke boldly (Moses and Esther).
- Pray for courage and wisdom before addressing difficult topics.
- Use Scripture as a foundation for your message and conversation.
- Approach conversations with love and respect; exemplify Jesus.
- Be prepared to face opposition, as boldness can lead to challenges.
- Seek guidance from the Holy Spirit to know when and how to speak.
- Encourage others to join you in speaking out for righteousness.
- Share personal testimonies to illustrate the impact of faith in action.
- Remain steadfast in your convictions, trusting in God's support and guidance.

Journal Your Thoughts

In Order to Renounce Sin and Embrace Holiness

37

You Must...

"DEVELOP A DEEP HATRED OF THE WORLD"

In Order to Renounce Sin and Embrace Holiness

You must... "Develop a Deep Hatred of the World"
1 John 2:15

Developing a profound disdain for worldly values, as highlighted in 1 John 2:15, can serve as a powerful catalyst for renouncing sin and embracing a life of holiness. This Scripture warns against loving the world and its fleeting pleasures, urging believers to focus on a higher calling. When we cultivate a deep-seated aversion to the superficial allure of worldly desires, we begin to see them for what they truly are: distractions that lead us away from our spiritual purpose.

By recognizing the emptiness of materialism, fame, and transient pleasures, we can shift our focus toward what truly matters—our relationship with God and the pursuit of righteousness. This shift in perspective is crucial; it allows us to identify the temptations that once held sway over us and to reject them with conviction. The more we understand the destructive nature of sin and its consequences, the more we are motivated to seek a life that reflects God's holiness.

Moreover, this hatred for the world fosters a sense of urgency in our spiritual journey. It compels us to examine our lives critically, identifying areas where we may have compromised our values. As we grow in our disdain for worldly influences, we become more attuned to the voice of the Holy Spirit, guiding us toward a life that honors God. This process is not merely about avoidance; it's about actively pursuing a lifestyle that embodies love, kindness, and integrity.

In embracing holiness, we find true fulfillment that the world cannot offer. Our hearts become aligned with God's will, and we experience a profound sense of peace and purpose.

Ultimately, developing a deep hatred for the world is not about fostering negativity; rather, it is about liberating ourselves from the chains of sin and stepping into the light of a holy life, where we can truly thrive in our faith.

IN ORDER TO RENOUNCE SIN AND EMBRACE HOLINESS
YOU MUST... "DEVELOP A DEEP HATRED OF THE WORLD"

Here's an example...

One biblical character who displayed a deep hatred for the world and all that is ungodly is Lot, the nephew of Abraham. Lot's story is one of tension between his desire to prosper in a world filled with sin and his eventual deliverance from God's judgment. Lot lived in the city of Sodom, notorious for its wickedness and immorality, but he chose to settle there due to the fertile land and the material benefits it offered (Genesis 13:10-12). However, over time, Lot's heart became grieved by the wickedness that surrounded him.

In 2 Peter 2:7-8, the Apostle Peter speaks of Lot's distress, describing him as a righteous man who "was tormented in his righteous soul by the lawless deeds he saw and heard." Despite living in a corrupt society, Lot was deeply troubled by the sin and depravity he witnessed daily. He longed for something better and became increasingly uncomfortable with the prevailing culture.

Ultimately, God's judgment on Sodom and Gomorrah came, and Lot was rescued by angels. His story reveals a man who, despite his initial worldly choices, had a heart that rejected the corrupt values of his environment. Lot's life exemplifies the internal struggle of living in a sinful world while yearning for righteousness and deliverance from ungodliness.

Here's some practical steps...

- Understand the biblical definition of love for the world versus love for God.
- Reflect on 1 John 2:15-17, which warns against loving the world.
- Prioritize your relationship with God through prayer and Scripture study.
- Identify worldly influences in your life that distract you from God.
- Replace worldly pursuits with activities that foster spiritual growth.
- Cultivate a heart of gratitude for God's blessings to shift your focus.
- Engage in fellowship with other believers to strengthen your faith.
- Practice self-discipline to resist temptations that lead you away from God.
- Meditate on God's Word to deepen your understanding of His love.
- Commit to living a life that reflects God's values and teachings.

Journal Your Thoughts

In Order to Renounce Sin and Embrace Holiness

38

You Must...

"ADHERE TO THE DEMANDS OF MINISTRY"

In Order to Renounce Sin and Embrace Holiness

you must... "Adhere to the Demands of Ministry"
2 Corinthians 4:1-6

Adhering to the principles outlined in 2 Corinthians 4:1–6 can significantly aid in renouncing sin and embracing a life of holiness. This passage emphasizes the importance of integrity and the transformative power of the gospel. By understanding and applying these teachings, individuals can cultivate a deeper relationship with God, which naturally leads to a rejection of sinful behaviors.

First, the text reminds us that we have received mercy, which encourages us to live authentically and transparently. When we acknowledge the grace bestowed upon us, it becomes easier to let go of the guilt and shame that often accompany sin. This realization fosters a sense of gratitude and motivates us to pursue a life that reflects our commitment to holiness. By focusing on the mercy we have received, we can shift our perspective from one of condemnation to one of empowerment.

Moreover, the passage highlights the importance of not losing heart. In the face of challenges and temptations, maintaining a steadfast spirit is crucial. By relying on the strength that comes from God, we can resist the allure of sin. This resilience is rooted in the understanding that our struggles are not in vain; they are part of a greater purpose. Embracing this mindset allows us to view our journey toward holiness as a rewarding endeavor rather than a burdensome task.

Additionally, the call to proclaim the light of the gospel serves as a powerful reminder of our mission. When we actively share the message of Christ, we not only reinforce our own faith but also inspire others to seek holiness. This communal aspect of faith encourages accountability and support, making it easier to renounce sin collectively.

In conclusion, adhering to the teachings of 2 Corinthians 4:1–6 equips us with the tools necessary to reject sin and pursue holiness. By embracing mercy, maintaining resilience, and actively sharing the gospel, we can transform our lives and reflect the light of Christ in a world that desperately needs it.

In Order to Renounce Sin and Embrace Holiness
you must... "Adhere to the Demands of Ministry"

Here's an example...

One biblical character who strictly and firmly adhered to the demands of ministry is Elisha, the prophet who succeeded Elijah. Elisha's life and ministry were marked by unwavering commitment to God's call, and he showed a remarkable devotion to the prophetic office. When Elisha was called by Elijah to follow him, he immediately left behind his former life as a wealthy farmer, slaughtering his oxen and burning his plow to demonstrate his total dedication (1 Kings 19:19-21). This act of radical obedience illustrated his willingness to forsake everything for the sake of God's mission.

Elisha's ministry was characterized by strict adherence to God's commands, as he performed miracles, rebuked kings, and offered guidance to the nation of Israel. He demonstrated an uncompromising commitment to the Word of the Lord, even in the face of great opposition or personal sacrifice. Elisha's interactions with the kings of Israel, such as his bold confrontation of King Jehoram (2 Kings 3:13-14), show his unyielding stand for righteousness, despite the challenges of working with leaders who were often ungodly.

Through Elisha's life, we see a model of devotion to God's calling and the willingness to stay faithful to the demands of ministry, no matter the cost. His unwavering service continues to inspire those in ministry today.

Here's some practical steps...

- Explore the biblical principles that guide effective ministry.
- Identify key scriptural passages that outline ministry responsibilities.
- Discuss the importance of prayer and spiritual preparation in ministry.
- Emphasize the role of service and humility as taught in the Bible.
- Highlight the significance of community and fellowship in ministry work.
- Examine the need for sound doctrine and teaching in fulfilling ministry roles.
- Address the importance of accountability and mentorship in ministry.
- Encourage the practice of love and compassion as central to ministry efforts.
- Reflect on the call to evangelism and spreading the Gospel message.
- Consider the impact of personal integrity in ministry leadership.

Journal Your Thoughts

IN ORDER TO RENOUNCE SIN AND EMBRACE HOLINESS

39

You Must...

"RESIST DESPISING STRUGGLES"

In Order to Renounce Sin and Embrace Holiness

you must... "Resist Despising Struggles"

James 1:2-4

Embracing our struggles, as emphasized in James 1:2–4, offers a powerful way to turn away from sin and pursue holiness. When we encounter challenges, we stand at a pivotal moment: we can either give in to hopelessness or rise to the challenge, allowing our experiences to mold us into more resilient individuals. By welcoming these difficulties, we create space for personal growth and spiritual development.

Struggles act as a refining fire for our faith. They test our determination and unveil our true selves. When faced with adversity, we have the chance to examine our actions and decisions. This introspection can deepen our awareness of our vulnerabilities and the tendencies that lead us astray. Rather than seeing struggles as mere hindrances, we can recognize them as sacred chances for growth. Each trial we encounter imparts essential lessons about patience, endurance, and our reliance on God.

Additionally, embracing struggles nurtures humility within us. It serves as a reminder that we do not control everything and that we require divine support to navigate life's challenges. This humility can inspire a more earnest pursuit of holiness, as we become aware of our need for God's grace. Acknowledging our struggles makes us more likely to turn away from sinful habits that may have previously held us captive. We become more receptive to the guidance of the Holy Spirit, leading us toward righteousness.

Furthermore, the process of embracing struggles can enhance our empathy and compassion. As we face our own hardships, we develop a greater sensitivity to the challenges others endure. This newfound understanding can drive us to uplift those around us, creating a community that promotes holiness over sin.

Ultimately, by valuing our struggles, we can transform them into stepping stones that lead to a deeper connection with God and a life characterized by holiness. Embrace your struggles; they are the gateway to spiritual growth and renewal.

In Order to Renounce Sin and Embrace Holiness
you must... "Resist Despising Struggles"

Here's an example...

One biblical character who did not despise struggles is Sarah, the wife of Abraham and mother of Isaac. Sarah's life was marked by long periods of waiting, barrenness, and uncertainty, yet she did not despise the struggles she faced. From the beginning, Sarah's journey was filled with challenges, particularly the inability to conceive a child. Despite her advanced age and the years of longing, Sarah held onto God's promise, even though it was difficult to understand or believe at times.

When God promised Abraham that he would be the father of many nations, Sarah struggled with doubt. In Genesis 18:12, she laughed in disbelief when overhearing the angelic announcement that she would have a son. However, despite her initial skepticism, Sarah eventually trusted God's plan. In Hebrews 11:11, she is commended for her faith: "By faith Sarah herself received power to conceive, even when she was past the age, since she considered him faithful who had promised."

Sarah's story is a testament to perseverance and the eventual triumph of faith over doubt. She did not despise the years of struggle but grew through them, learning to trust in God's timing. Her ultimate joy came in the birth of Isaac, demonstrating that even in the midst of prolonged trials, God's plans prevail.

Here's some practical steps...

- Understand that struggles are a part of life and can lead to spiritual growth.
- Read Jms. 1:2-4 and be encouraged to consider trials as opportunities for joy.
- Recognize that challenges can develop perseverance and strengthen faith.
- Embrace the idea that God uses struggles purposefully.
- Pray for wisdom and strength during difficult times, seeking God's guidance.
- Remember that Jesus faced struggles and set an example of enduring faith.
- Share experiences with others to foster community and support.
- Keep a journal to document struggles and the lessons learned from them.
- Focus on the hope and future promises found in Scripture.
- Cultivate a mindset of gratitude.

Journal Your Thoughts

IN ORDER TO RENOUNCE SIN AND EMBRACE HOLINESS

40

You Must...

"STAND FIRM"

In Order to Renounce Sin and Embrace Holiness
you must... "Stand Firm"
Galatians 5:1

Standing firm in faith, as outlined in the Holy Bible, is a powerful way to renounce sin and embrace holiness. The Scriptures provide us with a clear roadmap for this journey. In Galatians 5:1, we are reminded that Christ has set us free, urging us to stand firm and not be burdened again by a yoke of slavery. This freedom is not just a release from sin but an invitation to live in the fullness of God's grace. By standing firm in this freedom, we can resist the temptations that lead us back into sin.

Ephesians 6:14-16 emphasizes the importance of spiritual armor, instructing us to stand firm with the belt of truth and the breastplate of righteousness. These elements are crucial in our battle against sin. The truth of God's Word equips us to discern right from wrong, while righteousness protects our hearts from the corrosive effects of sin. When we actively wear this armor, we are better prepared to face the challenges that threaten our commitment to holiness.

In 1 Corinthians 16:13, we are called to be on guard, stand firm in the faith, and be courageous and strong. This call to vigilance is essential in a world filled with distractions and temptations. By remaining steadfast in our faith, we cultivate a resilience that helps us reject sinful behaviors and attitudes.

Finally, 1 Corinthians 15:58 encourages us to be steadfast and immovable, always abounding in the work of the Lord. This commitment to God's work not only strengthens our resolve but also fills our lives with purpose and meaning. As we engage in acts of service and love, we find ourselves naturally distancing from sin and drawing closer to holiness.

In summary, standing firm according to biblical teachings empowers us to renounce sin and embrace a life of holiness, transforming our hearts and minds in the process.

In Order to Renounce Sin and Embrace Holiness
you must... "Stand Firm"

Here's an example...

One biblical character who stood firm in faith and on the promises of God is Caleb, one of the twelve spies sent by Moses to scout the land of Canaan. When the Israelites reached the edge of the Promised Land, Caleb, alongside Joshua, was one of the only two spies who brought back a positive report, encouraging the people to trust God's promise and take the land (Numbers 13-14). Despite the fear and doubts of the other ten spies, who saw the inhabitants of the land as giants and were discouraged, Caleb stood firm in his belief that God would give them victory.

In Numbers 14:24, God commended Caleb for his "different spirit" and his wholehearted following of the Lord. Even after forty years of wandering in the wilderness due to the people's unbelief, Caleb's faith remained unwavering. At the age of 85, when most of the original generation had passed away, Caleb still believed that God's promise of the land was for him. In Joshua 14:12, he boldly requested the mountainous region of Hebron, where giants still lived, trusting God to help him conquer it. Caleb's unshakeable faith and dependence on God's promises resulted in his receiving the land he had believed in from the start.

Caleb's life is a powerful example of standing firm in faith.

Here's some practical steps...

- Explore the concept of standing firm in faith as outlined in the Scriptures.
- Identify key biblical promises that provide strength and assurance.
- Discuss the importance of prayer in reinforcing faith in God's promises.
- Highlight examples of biblical figures who exemplified steadfast faith.
- Emphasize the role of community and fellowship in supporting faith.
- Encourage regular study of the Bible to deepen your understanding.
- Suggest practical ways to apply biblical teachings in daily life.
- Address the significance of worship and praise in maintaining faith.
- Offer strategies for overcoming doubt and challenges to faith.
- Concentrate on the eternal nature of God's promises.

Journal Your Thoughts

Perfecting Holiness

Paul writes, "Therefore, having these promises, beloved, let us cleanse ourselves from all defilement of flesh and spirit, perfecting holiness in the fear of God." This verse presents a powerful call to Christian growth and sanctification, highlighting two key elements: the need to purify ourselves from sin and the ongoing process of "perfecting holiness."

To fully grasp the significance of this verse, it's essential to understand the context in which it was written. Paul is addressing the Corinthian church, which was struggling with moral and spiritual issues. In 1 and 2 Corinthians, Paul urges believers to live lives set apart from sin, aligning their actions with the gospel they profess. In the preceding chapter, Paul emphasizes the promises of God and the grace given through Jesus Christ (2 Cor. 6:16-18), calling believers to recognize their identity as God's chosen people, distinct for His purposes. Therefore, 2 Corinthians 7:1 is a natural extension of this message: since believers are God's people, they are called to live in holiness.

Paul begins by urging believers to "cleanse ourselves from all defilement of flesh and spirit." The term "defilement" refers to spiritual impurity, moral contamination, or stain. While the Old Testament often linked defilement to ceremonial uncleanliness, Paul uses this imagery to address a deeper, spiritual truth. "Flesh" refers to our human nature, particularly sinful desires, while "spirit" speaks to our inner moral and spiritual life, including our attitudes and actions.

Sin taints both the physical and spiritual realms of the believer's life. Cleansing, in this sense, is an ongoing process of turning away from sinful behaviors, attitudes, and actions. It involves actively renouncing sin's influence, not just in outward actions but through an inner transformation that aligns with God's holiness. This cleansing is made possible by God's grace through Christ, but it also requires the believer's active participation through repentance, confession, and obedience.

The phrase "perfecting holiness" is central to this verse, referring to the continual process of sanctification in the believer's life. The Greek word for "perfecting" suggests bringing something to completion or maturity, working it out to its full potential. To "perfect holiness" is to practice holiness—pursuing a life that reflects the essence of God.

> *" To "perfect holiness" is to practice holiness— pursuing a life that reflects the essence of God.*

Holiness, in this context, is not just moral perfection but being set apart for God's purposes in every area of life—body, soul, and spirit. Paul is encouraging believers to engage in the ongoing journey of becoming more like Christ. Holiness is both a position (as believers are already sanctified in Christ) and a process (as they are progressively transformed into His image).

Paul also notes that we are to "perfect holiness in the fear of God." This phrase emphasizes the attitude that should guide our pursuit of holiness: the fear of God. This "fear" is not a paralyzing dread, but a deep reverence, awe, and respect for God's holiness. It involves recognizing God's sovereignty, righteousness, and holiness, and understanding the seriousness of living in a way that honors Him.

The fear of God is the motivating force behind sanctification. It is not the fear of punishment, but a reverent understanding of God's holiness and the cost of sin. This kind of fear encourages believers to strive for purity, recognizing their calling to reflect God's holy and righteous nature.

"Perfecting holiness" is not an immediate achievement but an ongoing process of sanctification—a lifelong journey of becoming more like Christ. Paul calls believers to pursue this journey with dedication, knowing that true holiness is only attained through God's grace and power. Just as an athlete trains for a race, believers are called to train themselves in godliness (1 Timothy 4:7-8), relying on God's grace while actively seeking a holy life through repentance, obedience, and the fear of God.

In conclusion, my prayer is that this book has helped you understand your responsibility, what that responsibility entails, and how to fulfill it. The call to renounce sin and embrace holiness is a lifelong journey, and you are now equipped to continue this path. Keep perfecting holiness!

About the Author
Dr. Marcus E. Turner

Dr. Turner has devoted three decades to Beulah Baptist Church, serving as its Pastor for 25 of those years. In this capacity, he provides spiritual guidance and support to a committed community of Christian believers.

An accomplished author on various theological topics, he has also presented his insights at numerous professional conferences and has made appearances on national platforms.

In addition to his pastoral work, Dr. Turner has over 30 years of experience as a knowledgeable real estate consultant. His genuine passion for real estate drives him to assist clients and agents in achieving their real estate objectives. He possesses the essential insight and expertise to effectively guide customers, clients, and agents through the complexities of the real estate market. He finds great fulfillment in following the legacy of his late father, Robert L. Turner, who dedicated his life to God, family, and the real estate profession.

Dr. Turner earned his Doctor of Ministry (D.Min) degree in 1999 and subsequently completed a Master of Business Administration (MBA) in 2009. He has been happily married to Minister Lisa Shenee' Phelps Turner for nearly 30 years and takes pride in being the father of four adult children.

Learn More...

Beulah Baptist Church
Washington, DC

Marcus E. Turner
Real Estate Professionals

ADDITIONAL COPIES

Order Here to Receive a
$2.99 Discount
on every copy ordered

A Charge to Keep: 40-Lesson Bible Study

SCAN CODE

www.ingramcontent.com/pod-product-compliance
Lightning Source LLC
LaVergne TN
LVHW051559070426
835507LV00021B/2654